"Control issues often control and confuse us as [...] help and hope!"

—CAROL KUYKENDALL
Author and speaker

"George H.W. Bush was asked at the end of his presidency what he thought his greatest achievement was. As I recall, he noted that he had five kids who all wanted to come home to visit. This book will help you raise kids who want to come home to visit when they're grown. It will also help you understand what you can and cannot accomplish as a parent—and go a long way toward keeping you sane."

—MAX ANDERS
Author, *New Christian's Handbook* and
30 Days to Understanding the Bible

"So many parents—with the best intentions—try to strong-arm their kids into being safe, successful, and spiritual. But that hurts the relationship, and rules without relationship lead to rebellion. Whether you're burned out by arguing or weary of 'rescuing' your teen from his own mistakes, Tim Sanford has a far better way. It's time to 'lose control'—and start enjoying your son or daughter again."

—JOSH D. MCDOWELL
Author and speaker

"This book is for everyone—because not only will you learn a lot about your teen, you'll learn about yourself as well. Tim Sanford has reset the bar on books to develop your relationship with your teen."

—JOE WHITE
Director, Kanakuk Camps
Author, *Sticking with Your Teen*

LOSING
CONTROL
&
LIKING IT

how to set your teen
(and yourself) free

TIM SANFORD, M.A.

Tyndale House Publishers, Inc., Carol Stream, Illinois

Library of Congress Cataloging-in-Publication Data
Sanford, Timothy L.
    Losing control and liking it : how to set your teen (and yourself) free / Tim Sanford.
        p. cm.
    Includes bibliographical references.
    ISBN-13: 978-1-58997-481-4
    ISBN-10: 1-58997-481-6
    1. Parent and teenager—Religious aspects—Christianity. 2. Parenting—Religious aspects—Christianity. 3. Child rearing—Religious aspects—Christianity. I. Title.
    BV4529.S34 2009
    248.8'45—dc22

                                                    2008028245

Printed in the United States of America
1 2 3 4 5 6 7 / 15 14 13 12 11 10 09

CONTENTS

Introduction 1

PART I: GETTING TOO MUCH OF A GRIP

1 Control: It's Not Your Department 7

2 The Real Job of Parenting 21

3 Why Teens (and Parents) Go Out of Control 35

4 Free Will: "You Have the Right to Remain Stupid" 45

PART II: CONTROL AND YOUR GOAL

5 HOLDers, TOSSers, GRABers, and FOLDers 59

6 Three Habits of Highly Controlling People 75

PART III: TURNING OFF THE POWER STRUGGLE

7 Dances of Influence 91

8 Rules of Engagement 103

9   When They Make You So Mad (and Vice Versa) 121

10   Intervention: When You Have to Step In 129

11   "But I'm 18!" 147

12   Bringing It All Home 167

Notes 179

INTRODUCTION

Raising two-year-olds is hard work.

Raising teenagers is hard work.

When I'm talking to a group of teenagers, I tell them raising parents is hard work, too.

As for two-year-olds, they require constant supervision and complete physical care—from changing diapers to making sure they don't feed your old VCR their morning oatmeal. Toddlers can't always use words effectively to tell you what they want or need. It takes a lot of time, energy, and your best powers of observation to identify their feelings and anticipate their next move—and stop them before they try to give the cat a bath.

With teenagers, it's different. They don't need or want your help getting dressed. They don't need you to feed or bathe them—though you may think they do at times! They're fairly self-sufficient, at least when they want to be. They can use language to express themselves, though they don't always choose to exercise that ability.

Yet in many ways teenagers tax your time, energy, and mental and emotional stability more than they did as infants or toddlers.

Why?

It has to do with control.

Think about all the things you can control with a young child. You can schedule and regulate bedtime and bath time. You can decide the type of food offered—though each toddler ultimately decides what stays in his or her mouth instead of being smeared on the face or spit out in a Technicolor rainbow. You can choose when and how your child is exposed to fresh air, playmates, learning opportunities, entertainment.

You can even push those "laugh buttons" with the right toy or tickle spot.

Now think of the areas of your teenager's life where you have little or no control—or where your efforts to exert control are met with resistance or outright rebellion.

Maybe you can relate to Margaret's story.

Her two boys are video game addicts. She's tried to set time limits, but now that they're older, they often stay up late playing online games.

As a single mom with a heavy workload, Margaret gets up at 5:00 every morning. She can't stay up all night and monitor the boys' activities. They promise to go to bed at a reasonable time, but sometimes she wakes up at midnight or 1:00 A.M. to find they're still awake and playing games.

They're not bad kids. They're not making a mess or lots of noise. When she yells at them in the wee hours to go to bed, they do.

But it doesn't change their behavior the next time. Margaret feels frustrated and helpless.

The possibilities for control-driven conflicts in parent-teen relationships seem endless. But the options for resolving them don't. Who has the final say on most of these life choices?

Ultimately, it's the teenager—as he or she reaches complete independence as an adult.

I'm not sure I like that answer, either. But it's the truth.

We parents may nod our heads at this fact. But often we fight it when it confronts us daily. We're desperate for our kids to turn out "right"—and convinced the key is controlling them.

It's not.

True, teenagers need just as much of our attention as they did when they were younger—whether or not they realize it. They require our time and input—but in different, more indirect ways.

That's easier said than done. It would be nice if you could get time off to study the subject for a year or two. Unfortunately, parents don't get sabbaticals just because their kids are growing up.

That's where this book comes in. Congratulations on choosing to dedicate some of your time—which I know you have so much of these days—to reading it and applying the principles it presents.

You might be wondering what I know about parenting, control, and teenagers. I'm the father of two grown children. I'm also a licensed professional counselor with 20 years of experience as a therapist working with teens and their parents. Before that I was in youth work, so I've been around teenagers for over 30 years. I don't claim to know everything, but I've learned a lot about what works—and what doesn't—when it comes to raising adolescents.

In that time I've discovered a key to understanding parent-teen relationships: coming to grips with the issue of control. That may sound obvious, but it's surprisingly hard to work out in daily interaction with our teens.

Control issues can be very tough on parents, resulting in the kinds of struggles that will be realistically addressed in the following pages. My goal is to help you understand and accept what you *can* control as well as what you *can't*.

I also want to make your job as a parent easier—not to give you a to-do list that will only make your life harder. I don't want to make you feel guilty over the things you're *not* doing. I want to help lighten your load as a dad or a mom, not make it heavier—to make parenting your teen a bit less confusing and less stressful.

Working toward that goal, I'll help you discover clear boundaries where control is concerned and explain the critical difference between control and influence. You'll be able to use the principles in almost any situation you encounter with your teenager, regardless of your personality types.

I've divided the book into three parts to keep it organized in your mind—and mine.

Part I looks at the reasons why control is such a flash point between parents and teens—the misconceptions, attitudes, and even biology that spark those notorious power struggles. We'll consider what a parent's real job description is—and isn't.

Part II is the heart of the book. You'll see how to balance control, influence, and responsibility. You'll find out what to do and when—including when to step back and do nothing.

Part III applies the principles of control and influence to situations in which you may find yourself. That would include making and enforcing rules, picking battles, getting outside help, and dealing with an "adult" teenager.

Just to clarify, though, this is not a *Five Ways to Get Your Teenager to Clean Up Her Room* book.

Sorry.

One girl, almost 18, told me confidently, "The floor's the largest shelf in my entire room—and I'm just trying to use it as efficiently as I can!"

That girl was one of mine.

So if your kid's room is messy, just pull the door closed.

Okay. Now that *that* problem is settled, let's move forward.

You're on your way to losing control of your teenager. If that occurs in the right way, you'll eventually find that your son or daughter has grown into an independent young adult.

And what parent wouldn't like that?

PART I

Getting Too Much of a Grip

ONE

Control: It's Not Your Department

As a therapist working with teenagers and their families, I've heard many a story from parents. Some of them go like these.

- Denise's daughter is overweight, and the two constantly battle over junk food. While Denise serves low-calorie dinners and packs healthy lunches, she frequently finds her daughter sneaking between-meal cookies and chips. The 14-year-old spends her babysitting money at the nearby convenience store, loading up on snack cakes and soft drinks. Angry, Denise strikes back by withholding allowance and repeatedly warning of the consequences of unhealthy eating habits. Nothing seems to work.

- Mac's blood pressure skyrockets when he thinks of his 15-year-old son getting his driver's license in a few short months. The boy has completed an expensive, private driver-training course and seems cautious and responsible. But Mac can't stop remembering his son's kamikaze approach to theme-park bumper cars five years ago. This hapless father's knuckles turn white when his teenager is at the wheel; his right foot presses an invisible brake pedal while his heart races like crazy. He wonders if he should make his son wait to get his license until he's 17 . . . or 18 . . . or 20.

- Joe wonders where his little boy and girl have gone. His sweet, bright-eyed grade-schoolers suddenly have been replaced by a shaggy, lanky 15-year-old boy who appears unaware of his own overwhelming body odor—and a 13-year-old girl who favors tight tank tops and too much eye makeup. Joe's wife has had some loud conversations with their daughter about her tastes in clothes and cosmetics, but neither parent has confronted their son about his pungent smell. Joe knows it's probably up to him, but he hates to destroy the boy's self-esteem. He wonders whether he's just being a control freak. He looks on his bookshelf for help, but finds nothing. *They never deal with anything practical in those parenting books,* he thinks.

Like Denise, Mac, and Joe, you probably face plenty of situations in which a book called *The Complete Guide to Controlling Your Teenager* would seem helpful. It wouldn't be, though. The idea of being your son's or daughter's puppeteer might sound appealing, but the results would be disastrous for both of you.

This book takes a different approach. And when it comes to control, many of us parents need to as well.

Are You Out of Control?

Parenting is a daunting task when you consider the consequences of major decisions like these:

- how your teen spends his free time
- which friends she spends time with
- how he makes and spends money
- how she approaches her schoolwork
- when he starts driving
- what she eats, where she eats, and how much

- whether he goes to church or youth group
- what she looks like
- what level of personal hygiene he attains
- whether or not she uses foul language
- what parties and other social events he attends
- whether she smokes, drinks, or uses illegal drugs

It's no wonder so many parents would like to control those decisions until the last possible second. But is that wise, not to mention doable? Here are some questions you may be asking about control as you try to set boundaries with your teenager:

- Which parts of a situation belong to me and which belong to my teen?
- What's mine to decide and what's not?
- How much "rope" can I give my daughter before she "hangs" herself?
- What does my son get to choose, and what do I choose for him?
- Should I make my teenager go to church with the family?
- What about rules?
- What about freedom?
- What about being responsible?
- What about respect?
- What about his hair?
- How do I get her to do her homework?
- What if my daughter is already 18 years old?

Over and over I've heard parents ask questions like these. Control is one of the biggest issues they encounter, and one of the most misunderstood.

Illusions of Control

I try to base all my counseling on what Jesus said in John 8:32: "Then you will know the truth, and the truth will set you free." Jesus was talking about a particular truth—who He is as the Son of God. But I believe His observation applies to all reality. Knowing and understanding the truth—what reality actually is, like it or not—can set you free from the problems that come with lies and mistaken perceptions.

Error, wrong thinking, skewed beliefs, and misconceptions lie at the root of many, if not most, conflicts. That's certainly true of control. The more accurately you think about something, the healthier your life will be. The converse is also true. The more inaccurate your thinking, the more dysfunctional your relationship with your teen will be—even if you assume your thinking is fine, which we all usually do.

So here's a good place to start: thinking more accurately about control, in order to undo common confusion about its role in relationships.

Many tensions between parents and teens boil down to the issue of control. Sometimes it's not visible on the surface, but lurks below. For instance, you may think you're pressuring your son or daughter to work harder in school to have a better chance at college scholarships. But the deeper issue may be how you feel about the way your teen spends time—texting from that iPhone or hanging with friends instead of doing homework. The two of you are battling for the right to decide.

There are as many myths about control as there are days of the year. Our culture doesn't make it any easier; an alien visiting our society might think we're all a bunch of control freaks. Consider the phrases we use that have the word *control* in them. Here's a starter list:

- remote control
- quality control
- cruise control
- climate control
- traffic control
- crowd control
- master control
- weight control
- arms control

We talk about controlling our destinies, our lives; we study ways to control the aging process; we attend expensive seminars in an effort to control our eating habits, anger, financial future, thinking, moods . . . and children.

Self-help books and workshops—in the Christian arena as well as the general market—promise control. Much of the psychology practiced in the U.S.—cognitive behavioral therapy—focuses on control, too.

Don't get me wrong. The idea of having control is not bad in itself. Therapy that focuses on what you can *legitimately* control, as well as what you *can't*, is a healing and helpful tool.

But a person's fixation on needing control, which I often observe as a therapist, and the illusion that you need or have more control than you actually do, turn healthy ownership into a control-freak thing.

Most of us want control, plain and simple—and the more the better, thank you very much! That's because when we have control, we can make things turn out the way we want. We can be happy and avoid pain or displeasure.

If only it were that easy.

High-control people believe the best way to avoid pain is to keep a tight rein on the things around them—including key people, especially their children. After all, there can be a whole lot of hurt when children go astray.

I met such an over-controlling parent many years ago when I worked at a psychiatric hospital. I was the primary therapist for a teenage girl from a military family. She was rebelling, skipping school, experimenting with alcohol. Her family diagnosed her as a "behavior problem."

In our second weekly family therapy session, the girl's father—a high-ranking officer—stated emphatically that the only reason something goes wrong is because somebody didn't do his or her job correctly. Therefore, that somebody is at fault. He was referring to his teenage daughter, of course; everything else was under his control.

This father had an exaggerated sense of control, and a huge

misconception about it. He'd carried his "systems checklist" mentality home from the office, refusing to see that there were some things he couldn't control. He also refused to see that his campaign to over-control his daughter was partially—though not completely—to blame for her rebellion. Her behavior was an attempt to escape his overcontrol.

When you think of control, you might have visions of someone like this father—or a power-mad villain from an old James Bond movie. While I've met a few who could have been cast for such a part, the vast majority of us parents are much more "normal" in our desire for control. But because our culture encourages us to seek control—and because some Christians overemphasize its role in parenting—it's important to look at the way you think about the topic.

Everyone Has "Control Issues"

Most parents don't behave as extremely as the aforementioned dad. But that doesn't mean they have no problems with control. It's not an "all or nothing" proposition.

Take, for example, the issue of trying to "guarantee" what will happen to our children.

My early years were spent as a missionary's kid in Ecuador. In that culture there was a life philosophy that could be summarized as *"Que sera, sera"*—"What will be, will be." There was no "I am the captain of my fate and the master of my soul" quoted at graduation ceremonies.

As a result, I've come to see the truth in the following observation:

- You can drive the safest car built in the world (control).
- You can place your infant in the safest car seat manufactured (control).
- You can be the safest driver in your state, with all the necessary skills for every possible situation (control).
- Yet a drunk driver can still cross the double yellow line, hit you head-on, and take the life of your baby.

"Que sera, sera."

Where is your control now?

You were very wise and responsible. You did everything correctly. You controlled the things that were yours to control. But after all was said and done, there was no *guarantee* that you could keep your child safe. There were a lot of elements—including people—you couldn't control, yet which could have a huge impact on you.

"But I want a guarantee!" you may plead.

You're not alone. As parents, we want certainty that we can keep our children safe and raise them so they'll turn out well, following scriptural guidance.

But there is no guarantee.

"That kind of thinking is negative and scary! I don't like that."

Yes, it is scary.

"But what about the verse that says, 'Train a child in the way he should go, and when he is old he will not turn from it'?"

Proverbs 22:6 communicates a very wise *principle*. But it's not a *guarantee* that magically or spiritually overrides your teenager's free will—which, by the way, was given to him or her by God Himself. This biblical principle does not obligate God to you or force Him to make your teenager turn out the way you think he or she should.

"But—"

I hear you.

We parents want control so badly because we think that if we do the right things, our kids will turn out the way we want them to. It doesn't matter whether we're Christians, or whether we're "high-control" people or think we have no control at all. We still want it.

We want to be able to lay our heads on our pillows at night, with our teenagers snugly tucked into their clean beds, and know we did it "right."

Since there aren't any guarantees, many parents settle for illusions of control. An illusion often is more comforting than the truth. That may sound harsh, but I've found in my years as a therapist that most people have a hard time with the truth.

Reality can be a hard pill to swallow. But last time I checked, whenever you fight reality you lose.

That's just the way life is. Reality wins.

The only absolute assurance, for those who have a relationship with God through Christ, is that eventually they'll enjoy life forever with the One who made and redeemed them. *That's* guaranteed.

The rest of life isn't.

Ask parents who've lost a son or daughter to an automobile accident on the way home from a church meeting, or in a rock climbing fall, or to the sudden onset of cancer, or in a school shooting incident, about guarantees. See what they have to say about control.

I know parents like these. I've looked into their tear-filled eyes and attempted to field the "Why?" questions. Maybe you are one. If so, I'm truly sorry.

No Control?

Does this mean our lives are careening, like cars with the brake lines cut, toward the edge of a cliff? Should we just take our hands off the wheel and brace for the crash? Why try to guide our teenagers at all?

Keep in mind that there are degrees of control. While you can't guarantee the outcome, you *can* make a baby safer with a good car seat.

There are also different kinds of control: the kind that is *actually yours* to exercise and the kind that *isn't*. The key in parenting is knowing which is which—and knowing what to do with each.

You need to *keep and use* the control you're entitled to—or take hold of it if you've lost it.

And you want to *lose* the control you really don't have in the first place—and give up illusions you may have about it.

It's not easy to figure out! But that's why you have this book. It explains what's truly yours to control—and helps you quit trying to grasp control that doesn't belong to you.

Believe it or not, when it comes to raising teenagers, losing control can be a wonderful and freeing thing!

Your Brain and Control

To understand your assumptions about control, it helps to understand what you've been telling yourself about it. Your need to control grows out of your experiences, and how they affect your thinking and decision-making.

The neurology of your brain is complex, but for the moment let's compare it to a jukebox.

I mean a real jukebox, not a digital one—the old kind with vinyl 45s inside and a panel of buttons, each corresponding to a hit single. You watch as the record drops onto the turntable, the arm swings over, and the needle slips into the grooves to play your selection. If you have teenagers, maybe you can remember when these weren't called antiques!

That's what your brain is like. Each "record" has etched on it a simple, short phrase known as a belief. A belief is a statement of what you think is fact. Most of your beliefs were recorded, catalogued, and filed in your jukebox during the first seven to ten years of your life.

When you hear the word *belief,* you may think first of religious beliefs. But you have beliefs about every subject under the sun. You use them every day as you try to make sense of life. They're your worldview—all on a bunch of 45s!

So your thought process plays out (no pun intended) in the following sequence:

1. A new experience happens, or a series of similar experiences. Perhaps a bully trips you in the school cafeteria, and you land in the middle of your own mashed potatoes. Or you feel guilty while reading a "how to raise a teenager" book.

2. You attempt to understand this situation as best you can.

3. You draw a conclusion from the experience. It may be based on incomplete information available at that moment, but you assume your conclusion is true.

4. A recording of your conclusion is made into a belief statement and filed in your jukebox. The new record is polished, catalogued, and ready for future reference.

5. Every time a similar situation arises, that record plays. You respond according to the belief it contains.

We all have one record that sounds pretty much the same. It says, "All my records, all my beliefs, are true. I can even validate them with life experiences if I have to!"

We're quite defensive about our record collections. If you disagree with me, my defenses shout, "What do you think I am? Stupid? I wouldn't believe a lie! I'm intelligent! I know what's right and true, and I can back it up!"

If you're willing to drop those defenses, you may find some of your records are a bit warped. Some conclusions you've drawn about walking in the school cafeteria may have been based on incomplete information. What you read in that parenting book may be partly true, but may not be the best advice for you and your situation.

Remember, most of your records were forged in your first seven to ten years—long before you ever thought of raising a teenager. Your beliefs about things like love and discipline—and control—may not be totally accurate.

There are plenty of books for Christians that tell you what you should have on your records. But I want to encourage you to think deeply about the "control songs" your jukebox is *already* playing and whether they're true.

It matters because those records remain in the slots of your jukebox, some of them warped and misleading, waiting to be activated when life "pushes your buttons." When one of them plays, it may sound funny to everyone but you. To you, it sounds true. Most of us, after all, never stop to question our beliefs; we just believe them.

Some of your records may need to be remixed, updated, even tossed. This book will help you do that with records that revolve (so to speak) around the subject of control.

Many of us have whole albums on that subject. One of yours probably features the hit single about how every parent's job is to make sure his or her children turn out "right." Even though most of us don't quite know what that standard means, we feel obliged to meet it.

Oh, how wrong that record is.

If it were true, it would mean God messed up.

Control: A Reality Check

In Genesis we read about a place called the Garden of Eden. It was a perfect environment, a perfect "home."

In this perfect place there were two perfect people—God's children, Adam and Eve. Wouldn't that be nice to have perfect children?

And there was a perfect God—the perfect parent.

There was also a rule: "You must not eat from the tree of the knowledge of good and evil, for when you eat of it you will surely die" (Genesis 2:17).

You've probably heard the rest of the story.

Adam and Eve chose foolishly, defying what God had told them. Our human decay and ultimate death are stark reminders of that wrong choice—made by perfect people in a perfect environment with a perfect parent.

So what did *God* do wrong? If He "trained them in the way they should go," why did Adam and Eve choose the other option? If Proverbs 22:6 is a *guarantee* of success for parents, why wasn't it a *guarantee* for the Author of the Book?

Enter free will.

I'm talking about a God-given freedom to choose—part of being created in His image. Adam and Eve exercised it, and your teenagers exercise it today.

"But I *want* them to turn out right," you say.

Yes. I agree with you. But that's not your job.

"But I want the best for them, for *their* sakes."

I won't argue with that. But it's still not your job to make sure they do.

"But—"

I know. I'm a parent, too.

You do have a job, which I'll get to in the next chapter; it's just not *that* one. You could do everything exactly "right" all 18 years of your child's life under your roof—assuming you could know what "exactly right" was—and he or she could still choose "wrong."

God has given our children the option to be foolish, even to sin.

He doesn't *want* them to be foolish or to sin. But they're free moral agents to pick right or wrong, wisdom or folly, truth or lies, righteousness or evil.

To a parent, that's scary news. There really is a whole lot more that you *can't* control than you *can* control.

But before you get too discouraged, rest assured that we'll get to the topic of *influence*—of which you have a great amount with your children. You are *not* powerless as the parent of a teenager.

For now, though, I want you to go back and read the fine print on the bottom of that contract—the one you signed when you became a parent, the one that includes the possibility of having your heart broken.

"I never signed up for that," you might say.

But that's exactly what you did. You opened your heart to the possibility that it would be broken by the very child you love and want the best for.

You signed up to raise a little person—one for whom you're responsible but are not able to control.

So before we go on, take time right now (yes, I mean right now, or you probably won't do it at all) to contemplate the powerful words of "The Serenity Prayer."

It may be familiar. You even may have it memorized. But as you reflect on it this time, don't do it as an abstraction or for somebody else's benefit. Do it practically, for yourself as the parent of a teenager. Make it a personal prayer from your heart to God.

THE SERENITY PRAYER

God grant me the serenity
To accept the things I cannot change;
Courage to change the things I can;
And wisdom to know the difference.
Living one day at a time;
Enjoying one moment at a time;
Accepting hardships as the pathway to peace;
Taking, as He did, this sinful world
As it is, not as I would have it;
Trusting that He will make all things right
If I surrender to His will;
That I may be reasonably happy in this life
And supremely happy with Him
Forever in the next.[1]

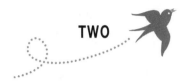

TWO

The Real Job
of Parenting

If controlling your teenager isn't your job, what is?

Before we go further, we need to figure out what your *real* calling is—to help you stop doing what *isn't* your assignment. A blurry job description makes it easy to wander into the overcontrolling side of the delicate balance between control and influence.

Your essential task depends on whether you're a mom or a dad. If that sounds like stereotyping, bear with me. I'm not talking about aprons and rolling pins and dragging cavewomen by the hair. I'm talking about doing what you tend to do best, and what your teen tends to need most from you.

What Dads Do

A dad's primary, underlying job isn't control. It's to *validate* every one of his children.

To validate means to let your child know over and over and over, through words and actions, that the following are true:

- "Hey, you exist and you matter to me."
- "You're good enough."
- "You're an okay kid."

Psychotherapists sometimes talk about the *looking-glass-self principle*. It's the idea that children get their earliest, most lasting impressions of who they are from what's reflected back to them by their parents. These impressions become those "records" in the jukebox of your child's brain.

Let's say four-year-old Johnny walks into the room where his dad is reading the newspaper, and Dad doesn't confirm Johnny's presence. Dad doesn't say, "Good to see you, son!" He doesn't even say, "Don't bother me. Can't you see I'm trying to read?" Johnny may begin to doubt his own existence.

It's like the old, philosophical question: If a tree falls in the forest and there's nobody around to hear it, did it make a noise?

In Johnny's case, the answer is no. His existence hasn't been validated by any response. He interprets that to mean, *I'm not an okay person.* This may be a totally wrong interpretation; his dad may not believe this for a second about his son, but this is how Johnny—and most children—will interpret this scenario. That's the way children's brains operate.

That's often why children do bad things, as in these cases:

- Sixteen-year-old Jenny barely saw her dad, thanks to his 12-hour days and golfing habit. He did give her a new computer, though, and thought that would be enough to show her he loved her. She used it to post suggestive photos of herself on MySpace. When her mom found out and tipped off Dad, he went ballistic and banned Jenny from using the computer for the rest of the year.
- Fifteen-year-old Ace saw his math grade going down the tubes, so he figured out a way to cheat on the final. He was desperate for a good grade because his dad only seemed proud of him

when he did well in school. His cheating technique wasn't very practiced, though; he was caught and flunked the test and the course. As a result, Dad ruled that Ace would have to wait a whole year to take the driving lessons needed to get a license.

• Thirteen-year-old Bob remembered the fun he used to have playing chess with his dad. These days, though, Dad traveled all the time and buried himself in televised sports when he was home. Without asking, Bob borrowed his father's expensive chess set and took it to school for chess club. Somewhere along the way, he lost a few pieces. When he confessed, Dad yelled at him for being a "careless idiot." After that, Bob didn't think there was much chance the two would ever play chess again.

In all these cases, a failure to do his job led a father to "clamp down" and substitute control for validation. That's a substitution that doesn't work.

Note, too, that by misbehaving these kids got *some* response—even if it was negative. By acting out, teenagers can affirm they exist and that their existence has impact on the world around them. Their lives have made "ripples in the water," so to speak. They get *something* from their parents, even if it's punishment.

To avoid that kind of acting out, remember: A teenager needs as much of your time and attention as a toddler does. In fact, a dad's validation is so critical to a child's emotional health that he or she will go to any length—and I do mean any—to get it, whether it's real or artificial.

Invalid Validation

What do you think of the following example? Does it fall under the definition of validation or not?

Jason wanted to play basketball, but he was no star athlete. In fact, he never shot baskets at home and barely dragged himself to practice for the YMCA team, frequently skipping at the slightest excuse. At home he whined to his dad about how hard the coach made the players work, demanding extra running drills.

When games started and Jason spent most of his time on the bench, he got frustrated and decided to quit. His dad felt sorry for the boy and told him it was all right to drop off the team.

"Some people just don't recognize natural talent," Dad assured Jason.

Is that validation?

And the answer is . . . no.

Validation doesn't mean lying. It doesn't mean telling me, "Great game, son!" when I really played poorly.

Many parents have so bought into the self-esteem movement that no matter who wins or loses the baseball tournament, everybody deserves a trophy. In a feeble attempt to "validate" every player (and assuming the only way to do that is with a shiny cup), we end up extracting the genuine power and intention of true validation.

Just as validation has nothing to do with control, it has no relation to being a "softie" as a parent. You can be firm and strong and still validate your child. It means acknowledging your son or daughter, certifying his or her *existence*, affirming the person apart from the not-so-good performance.

Some fathers go to the opposite extreme, withholding validation when kids don't "measure up." Our culture is so conditional in its validation—affirming only those who've won fame or fortune, or been born (or surgically assisted) with "good" looks—that the same approach often creeps into our parenting. It's easy for a man to validate a good performance; it takes a lot more time and energy to see and value the human being in the absence of any performance and put it into words.

In a way, these forms of "invalid validation" are another attempt to control the way our kids turn out. We want them to grow up full of confidence, so we give even mediocre performances rave reviews. Or we want them to achieve, so we skip the praise so they'll try harder to earn it.

A dad's biggest job is to relinquish that kind of control and affirm that the existence of each of his children, with or without any great (or poor) performance, is acceptable. If you're a father, recognize that each of your children is worthy of being alive. *You* may know that, but each of your children needs to hear it from you.

Value that child as a person, even when disciplining an action or attitude. Make sure your child knows he or she is good enough for you.

Otherwise, when that tree falls in the forest, the silence will be deafening.

The best time to begin validating is the day you bring your baby home from the hospital. Parenting a teenager begins when he or she is born.

When he or she is *born*. Really.

But it's never too late to start. Do it often enough to cut a record in your teen's jukebox that says, "I'm okay. I'm good enough." If you can do that, trying to compensate with control won't be such a temptation.

What Moms Do

What about a mom's primary job? It's not cooking dinner, changing diapers, or helping a preschooler glue colored macaroni on a coffee can as a Father's Day gift.

The most important assignment a mom has is to *nurture* her children.

But what does that mean, exactly? Most of us have a vague notion about what being nurtured feels like, but here are a few specifics.

A nurturing mom goes beyond being the "maintenance person" in a child's life. She doesn't just keep a child clean, fed, warm, and dry. She also helps enable her children to develop fully by pouring life into them. She models joy and passion. Nurturing is filling your child up with aliveness.

It's not a joyless, self-sacrificing caricature of Betty Crocker. A nurturing mom takes time to play, read, and take pictures when the toddler's spaghetti ends up on the head instead of in the mouth. She enters the child's world to see things from his or her perspective, even if it means the carpets don't get vacuumed for a while. She provides empathetic understanding from a position of strength and support. That's true whether she's dealing with a toddler or a teen—except for the part about spaghetti on the head.

Like dads, though, moms have a natural urge to protect their children. That can lead them to cross the line between nurturing and futile attempts at control. One mother of twins describes her ongoing battle with this issue:

> I remember when my boys were babies. I took them out for their first ride in the double stroller. Along the way, I saw a mean-looking dog running loose ahead of us. Instantly I made plans to save the lives of my children by throwing myself over their little bodies, suffering whatever injuries the dog's sharp teeth might inflict. When the harmless dog trotted away without any attempt to attack us, I laughed at how readily my "mommy radar" had me prepared to die for my kids, without thinking twice.
>
> Two years later, I struggled because it wasn't so easy to keep my little ones safe. As fast-moving toddlers, they were always three steps ahead of me at the lakeside park we visited often. Either I was chasing one down to keep him from following the geese into the lake, or I was wrestling my way up the jungle gym to spot my would-be mountain climber. But I didn't want to refuse my boys the pleasures of the playground and their freedom to explore. How often I wished to put each boy on a 200-foot leash so each could be free—within limits.
>
> Many years later, this struggle continues. I want my 16-year-olds to drive so they can enjoy the normal freedoms and growth of other teenagers. Yet I do what I can to instill the fear of death in them to keep them on a "leash" of careful driving

habits and away from daredevil maneuvers behind the wheel. Finding balance means continually going back and forth between the healthy desire to give my kids freedom and my God-given urge to keep them safe.

You can't control the results, but you can stir in the right ingredients. You can seek to know your children as individuals, different as they might be, and bring out the best in each. You can demonstrate by example how to explore life with zest and express the unique gifts God provides each of us. Your nurturing can blossom in emotional and spiritual growth.

Before you feel burdened with a mile-long list you can never follow through on, let me be quick to say that nurturing is not about "doing it all" or doing it perfectly. It's about doing the best you can—without losing yourself or driving yourself crazy because your own needs aren't taken care of. You won't be able to nurture your children if you're exhausted from burning the candle at both ends.

So please take care of yourself, too. *You* need aliveness in order to pass it on to your teenagers.

How Much Is Enough?

Validation from Dad, plus nurturing from Mom, equals "mission accomplished" as parents. You'll notice that the word *control* doesn't appear anywhere in that equation.

But speaking of equations, how much validation and nurture does your teenager need?

I've known teens praised for their accomplishments, but hardly ever validated for just existing.

I've known teens kept neat and clean and "mothered," but neglected and lacking those qualities needed to become fully alive as human beings.

Every person needs both validation and nurture to fully develop into a healthy adult. That's why God's ideal plan includes every child being raised by a mom and a dad. It doesn't always happen that way, of course, and I'll say more about that later in this chapter.

What happens when a child is raised in a home marked by too little validation or nurture or both? In my 20 years as a professional therapist, I've seen as many people in my office—if not more—who lacked these ingredients as I've seen who were abused by a parent. Don't get me wrong; abuse and neglect are very destructive. But the damage can be just as severe for those who didn't get enough validation from their dads or nurture from their moms.

I remember the story of a missionary kid in Ecuador. Though I've long forgotten the details, one statement from this boy—close to my age at the time—still rings in my ears. He said, "My dad will spend three hours talking to a drunk on a street curb, but he won't spend three minutes talking to me."

This boy was part of a missionary family, doing God's work in a foreign country. There was no abuse here—just lots and lots of "not enough." The damage was just as deep as if it had been caused by active abuse.

The pain, woundedness, and emptiness in case after case like this may be covered with a practiced smile or an impeccable résumé. But they're still there.

So how much is "enough"?

Do you have to be a perfect parent?

No, and no again!

Dad, your validation doesn't have to be flawless. It just needs to be *enough* for that individual child.

Mom, your nurturing doesn't have to be world-class, either. It needs to be *enough* for that particular child.

But how do you know what's "enough"?

Consider another word picture. Let's say you need 50 "units" of oxygen to stay alive. If you have 52, you have enough to live on—maybe not enough to run a marathon, but enough to survive.

If you have 96 units, you have enough—and some left over to climb Pikes Peak.

But if you only have 9 units, you don't have enough. You will die.

So if you have 49 units, do you have "enough"?

No.

"What are you bellyaching about?" someone might say. "You have a whole lot more than the person who only got 9!"

Some adults might say, "I know my parents loved me, and they gave me what little they could in the way of validation and nurture. I got more than a lot of other people did growing up."

But was it *enough*?

Some is not equal to *enough*.

"Enough" varies from child to child, personality to personality. What's enough for one child may not be for the next. If a child doesn't get enough validation and nurture, he or she may not physically die—but will be emotionally damaged and maybe even emotionally cease to exist.

That was the case with Angie. Sixteen years old, she was brought into my office because she was angry, hurting herself, and depressed. She came from an upper-middle-class "Christian family," to use her parents' words.

As I got to know Angie, she told me of the daily routine in her home. Dad was always busy with work, even when he was in the house, and rarely spoke a word to any family members. Mom was clinically depressed—nonfunctional in private, but upbeat and social when in the public eye.

There were no harsh words, no abuse, no molestation. Angie was just left to fend for herself—not because her chores were assigned, but because they wouldn't get done otherwise. She did her own laundry, made her own meals, checked her own homework, paid for her own things, and answered her own questions about life.

Yes, she was angry; she was all alone. There was no validation, no nurturing—no "fussing." Yes, she was harming herself; she was taking her anger out on the person she thought was at fault. She told me it was her fault for being born—a tragic jukebox record she'd been playing for years. And yes, she was depressed; you'd be depressed, too, if that were your life.

It was all because she hadn't gotten, and wasn't getting, enough validation and nurture—at least for her.

This story breaks my heart as I recount it. Angie chose illicit drugs rather than therapy to deal with her situation, and I never heard from her again.

Her story isn't unique, either.

This is not a call to "blame the parents for all the teenager's problems." It's a statement of reality and truth.

That's the vital nature of validation and nurture. Unfortunately, the necessity of both may be forgotten until after a child has been raised—often by moms and dads who spent their parenting years searching in vain for control.

What Makes It Hard to Do Your Job

Your job description *is* doable.

You *can* validate and you *can* nurture.

That's not to say, of course, that people and events won't conspire to make your job harder. Here are some factors that can make it tough to validate, nurture, and keep your fingers off the "control" button.

1. *The judgment of other parents.* It's easy to talk about other parents, evaluating their parenting based on how their teenagers are choosing and behaving. Since moms are often more closely tied to raising children than dads are, they're especially susceptible to this kind of talking, comparing, and evaluating.

Some parents even do this comparing in the "fellowship" halls of their own churches. Is that fellowship? Is it encouraging and uplifting? I don't think so.

The sad news is that it's so common. Have you been on the receiving end? Did you respond by trying harder to control your teen's behavior in order to silence the critics?

One lesson I've learned as a parent is to guard my mouth and not talk in an "evaluating" manner about another mom or dad. I've also learned to guard my heart when I hear others talking about me in that way.

Sure, it's easier said than done. But nobody said parenting was easy—just doable.

2. *Catching up*. When a child hasn't been sufficiently validated or nurtured, he or she can be thrown into an unconscious emotional "survival mode." This can put a record like the following on his or her mental turntable: "The only person in this whole world I can trust to look out for me is me. So I will do whatever I think I have to do to get my needs met."

If you think I'm talking only about a child adopted from an orphanage overseas, think again. Not getting enough validation or nurture can and does happen in our society, even among upper-middle-class, churchgoing, intact families.

These kids can be found on a continuum ranging from mild to extreme. Those on the mild end of the scale are often underdiagnosed and labeled as strong-willed, having attention deficit hyperactivity disorder, perfectionistic, "control freaks," lazy, underachievers, or just plain selfish.

While these may be partly accurate assessments, they don't tell the whole story. Attempts to help the teen "get his act together" will be met with limited success, because only surface issues are being addressed and not the underlying attachment and bonding problems.

Young people on the extreme end of this scale get noticed more quickly. Their negative behaviors usually are diagnosed as—among other things—oppositional defiant disorder, rebellion, antisocial behavior, or conduct disorder. Even if these diagnoses are correct, they still don't address the deeper issue of what's needed when validation or nurture is lacking.

Whether symptoms are mild or wild, the damage can be deep and severe. Professional therapy with a counselor familiar with bonding and attachment issues is in order.

3. *Single parenthood.* If you're a single parent, you may be facing a real battle.

Is that an understatement, or what?

I've said that dads are supposed to validate and moms are to nurture. Where does that leave you?

Mentors and other healthy role models can be very helpful, though most single parents I talk with say it's not easy to find such people for their teenagers. And finding them may not be enough. You and your teen may need to wear a path to a counselor's office—being sure to find a professional who has a working understanding of bonding and attachment issues with teenagers.

Melinda had been a single parent to her son for more than nine years when I met the two of them. Andy was now 13. During our first session I asked why they were talking to a therapist like me, since there seemed to be no real issues at hand.

Melinda explained that she just wanted a "checkup" for Andy and herself, to make sure they were both ready for the changes the teenage years would bring.

As the sessions progressed, it became apparent to me that this single mom had gotten it right. Yes, Andy was an "easy child" as far as personality goes. But Melinda had been purposeful in her parenting, and had kept Andy around spiritually solid men in the church through various activities. She'd given Andy enough nurturing and had done her best to see that he'd gotten as much validation as possible. The situation wasn't perfect, but for Andy it was *enough.*

There are many stories like Angie's—and many like Andy's, too.

If you're a single mom, you can nurture *and* validate your teen. If you're a single dad, you can nurture as well as validate.

Defining Success

Regardless of your parenting situation, you can erase "control" from your job description and add "validate and nurture." While you're at it, don't forget all that fine print about paying for things, coaching your daughter's soccer team, correcting your son's awful table manners, sitting through countless piano recitals, teaching spiritual values and how to balance a checkbook, driving all over town, disciplining, encouraging, saying no at times and yes at others, setting boundaries, and repeating all this as needed.

In doing this year after year, you greatly increase the opportunity for your teenager to choose what's wise and right. Even though you can't control the final outcome, you've stacked the deck in your child's favor. *That's* what your job as a parent is.

Get into the mind-set that everything you do as a parent ultimately is part of validating or nurturing your children, especially during their teen years—preferably in ways they don't consider offensive or embarrassing.

And don't forget that it's not about being perfect or exactly "right." It's about "enough."

Relax. You can do these things. And while there may be hard times, you can do them *successfully*, even if your teenager doesn't turn out "right"—now or later.

Remember, the results aren't in your hands.

The clearer you are about this job description, the more able you'll be to maintain a balanced approach to this thing called control.

THREE

Why Teens (and Parents)
Go Out of Control

Validating and nurturing your children are doable; they're on the list of
things you can control. But when it comes to daily interactions with
your teenager—where the rubber meets the road—we find a lot of
things that aren't. Consider the following examples:

- Jennifer is glad her 18-year-old daughter, Lisa, has the ambition
  to work a part-time job. But Jennifer worries about Lisa closing
  up the sandwich shop alone after dark. And though Lisa prom-
  ised the job wouldn't interfere with schoolwork, her grades are
  already slipping. Why can't Lisa be satisfied with babysitting,
  like in the good old days?

- Greg remembers a time when his son Jessie was thrilled to
  go on a weekend fishing trip. Now Greg's having trouble
  scheduling any time with his son. Jessie likes to spend Friday
  nights and Saturdays at a friend's house, playing video games
  with other teenage boys. Jessie's been getting sick more often
  lately; Greg thinks it's caused by lack of sleep and long nights
  in the friend's cold garage. Is it time to put a stop to these
  marathons?

- Louise has a huge headache. She let Ben go to the Sadie Hawkins Dance in spite of the tasteless T-shirt he wore. When Ben and his girlfriend said they were getting matching outfits for the event, Louise envisioned something classier than the blue shirt emblazoned with a vulgar joke. When she saw it on Ben just before he left to pick up his date, Louise told him to change it. He refused, and they had a huge argument. Finally she gave in, against her better judgment. From now on, will she have to inspect and approve his wardrobe every time he leaves the house?

If you don't see yourself in one of those case studies, no doubt you can think of recent examples that have caused conflict in your own home. Why is this happening?

Your teenager is in the process of moving away from you. Therapists have a term for this: *developmental individuating*. It means your child is doing the following:

- disconnecting
- leaving the nest
- launching out
- becoming his own person
- growing independent
- becoming a free moral agent

These phrases sound nice and inviting when they crop up on a psychology test covering the "developmental theories" chapter. But they don't always sound so positive and gentle when they're lived out in your family room or kitchen.

Still, the theory is right: Your teenager is separating from you and gravitating toward his or her peer group. This process is normal, natural, and necessary. Fight it and you'll lose. The solution is to work with it as well as you can—by understanding what's yours to control and what isn't.

They're Moving Out

Think of your son or daughter as traveling down a pathway toward maturity. All teenagers proceed along this journey, though at different speeds. As your teenager leaves the past behind, he or she moves toward the future and the changes it will bring. Let's look at some of those changes and the challenges they offer.

1. Your teenager is *moving away from parents and family and toward his or her peer group*. This is the "getting ready to leave the nest" process. Most 15-year-olds can't make it on their own in the adult world yet; they need opportunities to try, "fly solo," fail, practice, scare Mom, and fail again. All this trying can be very wearing on us as parents.

Your son or daughter also is connecting with his or her peer group, just as you probably did when you were that age. This is necessary to make life work; after all, these are the people your teenager will work with, work for, lead, follow, vote for, run against, buy from, sell to, marry, and bury. Your teen needs to find his or her niche within this group.

This quest is usually just as awkward for the teenager as it is for the parent. It must happen anyway, though. Being aware of it can at least lessen the stress and anxiety it can bring.

2. Your teenager is *moving away from dependence on you and toward being independent of you*. Notice I didn't say he or she necessarily is becoming *responsibly* independent. Research indicates your teenager will be dependent on your pocketbook—to some extent—on average until the age of 26.[1] This independent-yet-dependent stage can be prickly for both parent and young adult, especially when the latter doesn't want your involvement in her life but still needs your financial backing. That explains the bumper sticker I saw recently:

MONEY ISN'T EVERYTHING, BUT IT SURE KEEPS THE KIDS IN TOUCH.

3. Your teenager is *moving away from your rules and toward advice or counsel.* This is a struggle for many parents. Suggestions don't seem to have as much "bite" as rules do. Parents feel more powerful trying to enforce regulations than when they're simply giving advice, though the feeling is almost always an illusion. This movement by the teenager is also normal and necessary.

4. Your teenager is *moving away from your hands-on guidance and toward your hands-off availability.* It may not seem that way, especially when your teen still wants you to take care of those little tasks like laundry, cooking, cleaning, and paying for everything. And he does need your guidance in those "teachable moments" and when he wants answers to those "Oh, Mom, what about . . . ?" questions.

This kind of movement by a teen can be particularly difficult for a mom when her youngest child is moving away from the hands-on guiding she's been doing for years. For both moms and dads, the key phrase is "be there." Even if your teen doesn't always take advantage of your wisdom and knowledge and ideas, even if she doesn't even seem to want you around, be there—just in case.

5. Your teenager is *moving away from your control and toward influence.* I'll have more to say about the nature and impact of this shift in Chapter 7. For now, just realize that it happens.

Going with the Flow

The baton is being passed from you, the parent, to your teenager. This has to happen if he or she is going to be a healthy, adult human being. And it has to happen whether or not you think your teen is *ready* for it. It's easier to let go when you like the way your son or daughter is deciding and doing things. It's harder when you don't.

But it's not your job to make your child turn out "right," remember?

This disconnecting from parents, this preparing to leave the nest, is going to happen. It needs to happen, is *already* happening. So how can you work with it and not against it?

In some ways it's like one of my favorite activities, whitewater rafting. During years as a wilderness guide in Colorado, I learned that when you're in a little orange rubber raft, you'd better go with the flow. Don't try to paddle upstream; don't fight the current. Instead, use it to navigate through the rapids to your destination.

The key to staying upright is knowing that you don't have control over the river or its direction—but you *do* have control over your actions and placement of your raft. You work with the river; you go with the flow.

In the same way, you can learn to go with the flow of changes in your teenager. It's not easy or smooth; it usually happens faster than the parent is ready for and more slowly than the teenager thinks he's ready for. But you can go with the flow, and keep paddling, too.

Obstacles in the River

If whitewater rafting were just a matter of floating downstream, it wouldn't be much of an adventure. So it is with the journey to adulthood. Just as every interesting river contains rocks and waterfalls and "strainers" that threaten to trap you underwater, the path you and your teen are trying to navigate includes some hefty obstacles. Here are five that make it harder for parents to keep their fingers off the "control" button.

1. *Teen brains aren't finished yet.* When I get to this part of my lectures on parenting teens, teenagers look at me in disgust while parents nod their heads vigorously. That's because I present research revealing that the frontal lobe of the brain—the part responsible for decision-making and reasoning—isn't fully developed until a person's early 20s.

According to Abigail Baird of the Laboratory for Adolescent Studies at Dartmouth, the human brain continues to grow and change into the early 20s. "We as a society deem an individual at the age of 18 ready for adult responsibility," she states. "Yet recent evidence suggests that our neuropsychological development is many years from being complete."[2]

As a result of this physical reality, your teenager is caught between two worlds: that of being a child (with simple, incomplete thinking, and a minimal data bank of experience), and that of being an adult (with more complete, mature thinking and a bigger data bank).

Teenagers can and do act like adults at times. This is normal. And they can and do act childishly at times. This is also normal.

This aspect of neurology doesn't mean your teenager has an automatic excuse for wrong behavior or poor decision-making. But your relationship will be less troubled if you realize this yo-yo behavior and these thought patterns are to be expected—and that you'll have to deal with them.

2. *We're overstimulated.* We live in an overconnected society. You can take the entertainment industry wherever you go, fitting thousands of tunes and hundreds of video clips in your shirt pocket. You can surf the Internet on your cell phone—or just talk or text constantly on it. You don't have to miss a TV show, thanks to cable and dishes and the transformation of "Tivo" into a verb. You can claim "friends" you've never actually met through online gaming and social networking sites. The assault of advertising is endless, whether on a NASCAR vehicle, a shopping cart, a Jumbotron, a gas pump, or even a church bulletin.

Then there are the after-school sports, the scholarship contests, the oboe recitals, and the laser tag parties.

It's just too much.

What happens when you overstimulate a cricket or a grizzly bear? It gets aggressive. (I learned this from a documentary one night as I was attempting to surf the too-many channels we have on our cable service.) The same thing happens with human beings.

Too much of a good thing . . . is a bad thing. It's a formula for agitation, rudeness, being constantly "on edge." Overstimulation also drives impulsivity; that much data can't be processed. There's no time to *think*, so a person simply reacts. The result: poor decisions.

When you react on impulse, you're no longer in control of yourself. Not a good idea, whether you're a teen or a parent.

3. *We're tired.* The mayhem of modern life keeps many of us from getting enough rest. Sleep deprivation leads adults and teens to exhibit chronic mental and physical fatigue. It wears down a person's ability to reason. In extreme cases, it can lead to psychotic episodes.

How can you tell if you or your teenager is sleep-deprived? Just answer these questions:

- Do you have to use an alarm clock to wake up in the morning?
- Do you rely on stimulants like caffeine to get going in the morning and during the day?

If your answer is yes to either of these, you may be sleep deprived. Talk to your family physician about how you might handle that problem.

A little rest can make a big difference in family relationships. One couple that entered my office for marital therapy was obviously tired. Instead of assigning those spouses to read a book or do communication exercises, I asked them to take a vacation, say "no" to some activities, and not come back for several weeks. When they returned, we made great progress. As we finished our last session, the husband told me that first assignment was the best thing he'd ever heard—and that if I'd hit him instead with all the things he was supposed to do as a Christian husband, he'd have walked out and never returned.

Whatever happened to the idea of a day of rest—not as legalism but as a sanity-saver? What happened to going on a picnic in the park or taking an afternoon nap? Ignoring your need for rest affects the level at which you and your teenager exercise sound, wise control.

4. *Young adults have permission to stay irresponsible.* Due to the number of people in the workforce, your teen's generation might be considered unneeded. The workplace is already crowded and competitive, so there's no rush to bring young people aboard. This is one factor leading to the acceptance of a much longer stage of adolescence.

Time magazine reporter Lev Grossman studied this phenomenon of delayed adulthood and wrote, "Thirty years ago . . . the median age for an American woman to get married was 21. She had her first child at 22. Now it all takes longer. It's 25 for the wedding and 25 for baby. It appears to take young people longer to graduate from college, settle into careers and buy their first homes. What are they waiting for? Who are these permanent adolescents . . . and why can't they grow up?"[3]

Our culture grants teenagers permission *not* to grow up, *not* to be responsible, *not* to be mature. Many skirt responsibility for their finances, decisions, and behaviors—not to mention the idea of moving out on their own.

In short, your teenager is being encouraged to avoid independence while you're trying to guide him or her to be a responsible, independent adult. Can you hear the tension?

5. *The culture doesn't support your values.* "Growing up" isn't the only subject on which teens hear mixed messages. You might urge your kids to stay away from alcoholic beverages, while many sports celebrities pitch beer. Youth groups teach teens to abstain from sex before marriage, while TV shows present premarital sex as the norm.

This issue isn't new, and the tension between Christianity and culture has always existed. But the impact of overstimulation and the permission to remain immature make the problem much worse. Your teenager needs time to think things through and wrestle with his or her belief system—but time is in short supply. Faced with a constant barrage of contradictory messages, it's no wonder so many kids don't know how to grow mature and act wisely.

The Right Direction

You're not going to eliminate these obstacles by reading this book. But recognizing them gives you an advantage when assisting your teenager through these difficult years, now and in the future.

Remember, don't fight the river. Go with the flow. Paddle vigorously in the right direction.

Yes, the currents are making your job that much harder—and you can't control them. That's why it's vital not to lose control over the things that are rightfully yours—as a parent seeking to raise a responsible teenager to adulthood.

FOUR

Free Will: "You Have the Right to Remain Stupid"

Most of us want the best for our children. We do what we can to protect and care for them. But the time comes when we gradually release that grip and allow them to make their own decisions and taste the consequences of their actions—within reason.

This "letting go" takes place in many ways and in a variety of settings and stages. Some parents stop overseeing homework when their kids enter middle school, for instance—either because the kids have enough self-discipline to do the work or simply because the math problems get too complicated. The same thing happens as parents find themselves slowly granting more freedoms in dating, driving, clothing and hairstyle choices, use of free time, and more.

For one mother the act of letting go has been difficult, especially when it comes to trusting her son with her life and limb. She writes:

> Letting go of control, or acknowledging that I can't control my teenage son in many ways, is hard for me. And this struggle isn't lost on my 16-year-old, either. For example, while I know he is a cautious, careful kid, I still get nervous when he's driving with

me in the car. But he's been driving successfully to school for many months, and now he doesn't like it when he's at the wheel and I give him driving instructions—like I used to during his training phase.

Recently he was driving us along a busy street with lots of road work. The heavy traffic made me tense, so I urged Chris to slow down.

"Mom," he said with obvious irritation, "I've been driving myself for almost a year. I know when to stop."

Struggling to keep my comments to myself, I resorted to biting my tongue and pushing down on the invisible brake we all believe exists on the passenger sides of cars with teenage drivers.

Of course, Chris noticed the way I jerked my leg. "What are you doing?"

"Just stretching my leg," I replied, not exactly truthful, not exactly lying.

"It looked like you were hitting the brakes." His hurt, accusing tone showed how much he wanted my affirmation and trust in his driving skills.

"How could I be hitting the brake? There's no brake here." Yes, I barely sidestepped his accusation and changed the subject, commenting on what a capable driver he has become. I couldn't admit the "invisi-brake" was helping to keep my nerves under control.

We arrived safely at our destination, though I was sweat-soaked and spent. It's so much easier to let my boy drive when I'm not there to worry in front of him. Hiding all that concern takes a lot out of a mom. But I can't undermine his confidence by allowing him to believe I don't trust him.

Next time I plan to wear a really long skirt so he can't see my right foot pushing a hole in the car floor. These days, the invisi-brake is all I've got in the way of control.

Some parents aren't content with an invisible brake. One 14-year-old girl was convinced her father didn't love her and thought she was ugly. The reason? She'd dyed her gorgeous brown hair black with bright red streaks, leading him to criticize her relentlessly about the way her hair looked.

It was the only thing that father talked about with his daughter. His nonstop, insensitive efforts to control the way she looked didn't change her appearance. All he did was inflict deep wounds on the girl's self-esteem and on their relationship.

If you find yourself white-knuckled in your efforts to either control your teen or release control, you'll benefit from a broader view of the subject. Let's take a step back to consider some essential truths about control—way back to the Garden of Eden.

A Very Short Study on the Theology of Free Will

Relax. Even though I'm ordained as a minister, this won't turn into a theological primer on the sovereignty of God and the free will of man. I just want to start with three simple yes-or-no questions.

Imagine this dialogue between your basic theology student and the professor of the class.

"Is God sovereign?"

"Yes."

"Did God give each person a free will?"

"Yes."

"Sovereignty and free will. How does God orchestrate these seemingly opposing concepts in a balance of harmony and unity?"

"I don't know. But He is God, after all, and He can."

This may seem to have little to do with parental control, but it's at the heart of the issue.

You and I, and your teenager, make choices every day. Some of them have huge effects on our futures. What informs these choices? Does God control them? If not, who does?

> Then God said, "Let us make man in our image, in our likeness, and let them rule over the fish of the sea and the birds of the air, over the livestock, over all the earth, and over all the creatures that move along the ground." So God created man in his own image, in the image of God he created him; male and female he created them. (Genesis 1:26-27)

> The LORD God took the man and put him in the Garden of Eden to work it and take care of it. And the LORD God commanded the man, "You are free to eat from any tree in the garden; but you must not eat from the tree of the knowledge of good and evil, for when you eat of it you will surely die." (Genesis 2:15-17)

Fact #1: Adam and Eve were created as perfect beings and placed in a perfect environment.

Fact #2: They were given a rule: "Don't eat of that tree."

Fact #3: God was—and is—sovereign, all-knowing, and ever-present.

On that day described in Genesis 3, as God watched Adam and Eve walk toward the forbidden tree, heard them talking about the fruit, understood what they were about to do, knowing that the serpent was laying a trap for the whole human race—did He stop them?

No.

Why not?

Why didn't He jump out and ask Adam, "What have we talked about before?" Or maybe use a more straightforward tactic and say, "Freeze!"

Didn't God know what the consequences were? Didn't He care?

This is not something to be taken lightly, even if you're not a student of theology.

Just look at the consequences of that choice. Practically every human being ever born has died—or will die—because of it. God the Father chose to sacrifice His own Son, Jesus Christ, to redeem mankind—all because of that choice.

So, *why?*

Because each person is made in God's image. And part of that God-given image is the ability to choose. We are free moral agents.

If God had stopped Adam and Eve that day, He would have taken part of His image out of all people. They would follow God not of their own free choice but because there was no other option. No other option means no choice—not really.

God did not want to do that to the human race, so He let Adam and Eve choose—and let them choose *wrongly.*

For the record, God did not *make* Adam and Eve choose wrongly. He did not *want* them to do so. But, in His sovereignty, He *allowed* them to choose for themselves.

God gave that same free will to your teenager. Your teenager has the power to choose "smart." Or "stupid."

"But I don't want her to choose stupid!"

I understand.

Still, she does have the God-given opportunity to choose either way. She can choose smart or she can choose stupid. In the end, the choice is hers.

This is the wild card in our discussion of control. If you try to take your teenager's choice away—by threatening, begging, or using guilt tactics or any other form of manipulation—you're trying to do something God didn't and won't do. You're trying to take part of God's image out of your teenager.

It won't work, so don't try.

Several years ago I saw a bumper sticker that I wish I had today, and I'm a guy who's generally not into bumper stickers. It read,

> PEOPLE HAVE THE RIGHT TO BE STUPID.

The words were plain—and very true. You have the right to choose stupid. So do I. And your teenager does, too.

So what are parents to do? Give up? Let their kids make life-threatening mistakes like driving too fast or dating the wrong person? What?

I'm a boil-things-down-into-simple-terms sort of guy. In my years of working with young people and their parents, I've simplified my approach into what I call "The Three Rules of Life." Maybe they appear a little *too* simple, but they're a great place to start.

These rules aren't just for teenagers, by the way. They aren't just for moms and dads, either. If you're a human being, these rules are for you.

Rule One: You Live and Die by Your Own Choices

Yes, people and circumstances influence us. Things happen every day that we can't control. But we *do* control the choices we make in *response* to those circumstances and people. We all have choices, and we move in the direction of life or death with every choice we make.

This is usually the place in my parenting seminar where the rebellious teenager who was staring me down from the back row says, "Yeah, it's my life. Let me make my own choices!"

He's right.

But I smile, because I know Rules Two and Three are coming!

Rule Two: You Can Choose Smart or Stupid

Since you live and die by your choices (Rule One), the question is whether your choices will be smart or stupid.

Some choices are also *legal* versus *illegal* or *moral* versus *immoral*. But they all boil down to this basic question: Are you going to choose smart or stupid?

If Rule One roused the teenager in the back row out of his catatonic state, Rule Two gets his fire going. "Well, *I* don't think marijuana *should* be illegal," he says. "That's a stupid rule in the first place. Don't you know it has medicinal value?"

He's entitled to his opinion.

I smile again, and remind him ever so humbly that *he* doesn't choose which actions and behaviors go on the stupid list or the smart list. I also mention that *I* don't choose what goes on the lists, either—though we'd both like to be the list-makers, I'm sure!

The lists have been determined for all of us—by God's Word first and foremost, and society second. Natural consequences play a big part as well. Jumping off a high cliff might seem exciting while flying through the air at high speed, but the law of gravity insists such a choice goes on the stupid list. Every time.

So while a teenager doesn't get to choose what goes on each list, he does get to choose actions from the smart list or the stupid list. Just for the record, the illicit use of marijuana is on the stupid list—and the illegal list.

Rule Two gets a lot of arguments. Knowingly or not, we all want to personalize the lists to our liking and say it's God's idea.

For example, I took a counseling call one afternoon from a mother who'd told her son it would be "wrong" to take a two-week road trip with three of his buddies after they graduated from high school. She longed to add "road trip with buddies" to the stupid list and feel good about telling her son, "No, you can't go, because it's *wrong*."

I explained to this mom how behaviors get on the lists. To help her visualize this, I used the following target with three rings.

As I told this mom, we start with the bull's-eye, the innermost ring,

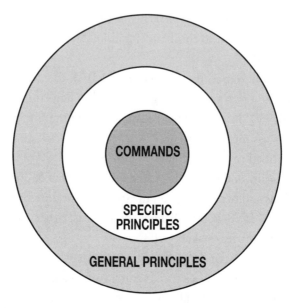

and ask this question: "Are there any *commands* in the Bible (clear, specific statements of 'do this' or 'don't do that') that speak to this situation?"

If so, then follow the command. That's how things get on the smart list. It's simple: Just do it.

In this case, is there a command that says, "Thou shalt not go on a road trip with your buddies after graduating"?

No.

So we move to the target's next ring and ask, "Are there any *specific principles* mentioned in Scripture that address this topic?"

If there are, then apply those principles as well as you can. These things are also on the smart list. Two people may apply the same principle differently, but in the Body of Christ we need to allow for some differences.

In the case of that worried mother, are there any specific principles in Scripture about taking a road trip with your buddies? Are there any proverbs, for instance, that say, "Unwise is he who travels the pathway with his friends"?

No.

So out to the final ring we go. We ask, "Are there any *general principles* in the Bible that shed light on this matter?" In this ring is the greatest room for differences in personal application.

If there are any general principles that speak to the situation at hand, apply them as well as you can. If some principles seem at first glance to contradict each other, balance them or consider which might best fit the situation. You might get others' input and counsel as well.

If there are no such general principles, ask God for wisdom and make your decision.

So, are there any general principles that speak to the idea of taking a road trip with your buddies?

Possibly. Here are some examples:

- The Book of Proverbs warns more than once to be careful about the company we keep and the circumstances in which we place ourselves. "Do not envy wicked men, do not desire their company" (Proverbs 24:1).
- We're admonished not to lead astray others who may have a weaker faith. "Be careful, however, that the exercise of your freedom does not become a stumbling block to the weak" (1 Corinthians 8:9).
- We're told that whatever we do, we should give it our all and do it to please God. "Whatever you do, work at it with all your heart, as working for the Lord, not for men" (Colossians 3:23).

So, was this mom on solid ground when she told her son that taking a road trip with his buddies was "wrong"?

No.

As we talked, it became clear that the real issue wasn't the road trip. It was that her son might choose *not* to be careful about the circumstances he allowed himself to be placed in. This mom was afraid he would choose stupid—and that she wouldn't be there to "make sure" he chose smart.

I mentioned to this mother that if her son wanted to choose stupid, he could do so without leaving their little town. I encouraged her to talk with her son about his freedom to decide, and the Three Rules of Life.

We're all entitled to our personal beliefs, opinions, and ways of applying biblical principles. There *are* commands laid out in the Scriptures, though there are fewer than some of us parents would like to acknowledge.

Rule Three: There's Always Somebody or Something Whose Job Is to Make Your Life Miserable When You Choose Stupid

Call it "cause and effect" or "reap what you sow"—it's true all the same. When you choose stupid, sooner or later that choice will come back to bite you. There's always an "ouch" to a stupid choice.

When your teenager chooses smart, he or she reaps the rewards.

When your teenager chooses stupid, he or she gets the "ouch."

This pain might come from you, a girlfriend or boyfriend, peers, a boss, or the gang across town. The "ouch" might take the form of an auto accident, losing a job, failing a class, getting arrested, or being grounded for a week.

While you can't make your teenager turn out "right," it *is* your job to reward smart choices and penalize stupid ones. That's life.

After all, if you live in the U.S. and try stupid (and probably illegal) financial tricks on your federal income taxes, it's the job of the Internal Revenue Service to make your life miserable, isn't it?

If you do stupid things behind the wheel of an automobile, it's the job of that police officer on the motorcycle to make your life a little miserable. You may not get caught at every stop sign you roll through, but the officer will nail you every time he sees you. The time lost, the fine paid, and the points marked against your license are all "ouches."

If you make stupid choices at your place of employment, you'll likely be made miserable by a boss or security guard. If you choose to park your Mustang convertible outside with the top down in Limon, Colorado, in the middle of a January blizzard, the elements will make your life miserable.

You get the idea. And so will your teenager if you convey a message like the following:

"And by the way, teenager of mine, one of my many jobs as your parent is to make your life a little miserable when you choose stupid. I can't choose on your behalf; Rule One says you live and die by your own choices. I can't make you choose smart—though I will unashamedly state that I'm encouraging you in that direction. But it's my job to make you 'ouch' a bit if and when you choose stupid."

Yes, It's Scary

That's the grown-up world. We adults live with the Three Rules of Life every day. What makes it extra scary for us as parents is that the rules are true for our kids as well.

- Your teenager will live and die by his or her choices, not by yours.
- Your teenager has the power to choose stupid as well as smart.
- You need to penalize poor choices, but life often does that anyway—and more harshly.

We long to keep our teens from making stupid choices. But God has given them the power to do just that.

That's life. It's reality. That's why I keep coming back to Jesus' words, "Then you will know the truth, and the truth will set you free" (John 8:32). When it comes to raising teenagers, the more your perceptions match reality the freer—and less frustrated—you'll be.

This is a part of life we parents need to learn to accept. "The Serenity Prayer" (see Chapter 1) reminds us "to accept the things I cannot change." It also points out that it's wise to know where the line between "can control" and "can't control" lies.

Learning this doesn't seem to come naturally. It's not an automatic response that kicks in when we have kids.

Don't give up on parenting your teen. Don't curl up in a tight little ball, feeling powerless and hiding under the kitchen table. Instead, embrace the reality that whatever you do as a parent, your teenager still has that gift of free will. You could do everything right and your teenager could *still* choose stupid.

That part is not your fault, even if it breaks your heart.

I've met parents who did things well, only to watch their kids go the way of stupid choices. It's nothing new. How many times do you think the father of the prodigal son (Luke 15:11-32) laid his head on his pillow with a knot in his stomach and an ache in his heart?

What *is* your job?

To validate and nurture.

What's *not* your job?

To make your teenager turn out right.

Learn to be content with these realities, and your life as a parent will be a lot easier.

PART II

Control and Your Goal

FIVE

HOLDers, TOSSers, GRABers, and FOLDers

It's true that contemporary culture makes your job as a parent more difficult. It's true that your teenager holds this wild card called free will.

But parenting is still doable. You just need to know what you *can* control and *can't* control.

Easy, right?

Well, no.

Lines can get fuzzy when your daughter has just stormed into her bedroom and slammed the door for the tenth time in one day. Or when your son calls to tell you he's "slightly" dented the car on a badly located street sign—and it *wasn't* his fault.

This chapter suggests how to draw some lines between "healthy" and "unhealthy" when it comes to control and your teenager. To understand these boundaries, you need to understand the terms *control* and *responsibility*.

Who's in Control?

There's an old saying: "People can be divided into two categories—those who divide people into categories, and those who don't." When it comes to raising teenagers, though, the world really *can* be split into two major categories:

Here *control* means *to have direct and complete power over.*

Given this definition, what in your life really fits into "What I Can Control"?

(Hint: The answer is *not* "nothing.")

You probably will come up with only three things: me, myself, and I. That's it. You control what you do, what you think and believe. You control your values, attitudes, and opinions, and how you express and manage your emotions.

You can control yourself. You cannot control other people, though you may be able to influence them. You can't control the weather or every part of any given circumstance. You just can't.

But there's always some *piece* of any given circumstance that you *do* have control over. It may not include as much control as you'd like, or any control over other people. While you can't control the situation, you can control your attitude and response.

Even if you have only the opportunity to choose between a rock and a hard place, there's always something you can control—because *you* are in the present situation, and you can control yourself. The key is finding that shred of control and exercising it.

If that's all that fits into the "What I Can Control" category, guess what fits into "What I Can't Control"?

Everything and everybody else.

That's a whole lot—over six billion human beings, not to mention events and pets. As a person and a parent you have lots of *influencing* power; but right now let's stick to the subject of control, because it's so hard for so many parents to figure out.

This prompts me to ask, "Do you like the way the world is divided up?"

"No!" you might say. "I don't want to control the whole world, but I'd like *more* control—especially over things that have a direct impact on me and the people I love."

I understand, but that's not reality. And one of those six billion humans you don't have control over is your teenager. Knowing this is the starting point of losing control of your teen and liking it.

If the only things you can control are "me, myself, and I," guess who has control over your teenager? He or she does.

Whether your teen exercises *wise* control is a whole other topic. But it's not your job to make sure (that is, *control* the outcome) that he or she turns out right. You can't do it anyway, so stop trying.

Who's Responsible?

Another way to categorize people and events is shown in the following diagram.

```
┌─────────────────────────────────────────┐
│                                         │
│                 WHAT                    │
│               I TAKE                    │
│            RESPONSIBILITY               │
│                 FOR                     │
│                                         │
├─────────────────────────────────────────┤
│                                         │
│                 WHAT                    │
│             I DON'T TAKE                │
│            RESPONSIBILITY               │
│                 FOR                     │
│                                         │
└─────────────────────────────────────────┘
```

Responsible is a compound word: *response-able*, meaning "able to respond." The only things you can legitimately respond to—the only things you can take "ownership" of—are the things you have control over.

This is not the same, by the way, as being *liable*. Liable means to be legally obligated to make good any loss or damage.

Consider this particular case.

Mark was a single parent with a 14-year-old daughter. She was extremely rebellious; that's why he brought her to see me. Mandy refused to cooperate with anything her dad tried to get her to do.

One night as Mark was sleeping—expecting his daughter would be doing the same—Mandy snuck out of the house. She took Mark's car, using a key she'd secretly copied weeks before from his backup set of keys. She drove to a friend's house.

Mandy was not an experienced driver, to say the least. She managed to get into a fairly colorful fender bender with a stationary vehicle.

The police were called; reports were made. Mark ended up at the police station, dealing with the consequences of his daughter's actions.

Now it's quiz time.

Question One: Was Mandy's "borrowing" the car something Mark could *control*?

Answer: No. For Mark, it belongs in the "What I Can't Control" category.

"But wait," you might say. "It was Mark's fault, because it was his car. I mean, if he didn't have a car, there would have been nothing for Mandy to 'borrow,' right? And if he didn't have an extra set of keys, it would have been harder to make a copy."

If you want to follow that logic—and we as parents often do follow a "logic" very close to this—then it was Henry Ford's fault. *He's* the one who mass-produced the automobile in the first place, at least in the U.S. If *Henry* hadn't done that, Mark probably wouldn't have had a car. Mandy wouldn't have had a vehicle to "borrow."

No, it isn't Henry's fault. It's not Mark's fault, either.

Question Two: Was the fender bender an action Mark was *responsible* for?

Answer: No. For Mark, it belongs in the "What I Don't Take Responsibility For" category. How could Mark have "responded" to the imminent crash when he wasn't even there? He wasn't response-able.

Question Three: Are the owners of the other vehicle going to go after Mark to pay for the damages incurred?

Answer: Yes. Mark, as Mandy's legal guardian, is *liable*. He is legally obligated to make good any loss or damage.

Mark can't *control* Mandy. He isn't *responsible* for the accident. But he's held *liable* for the damage. This is an awful catch-22 for us parents, but there seem to be tons of those throughout the teenage years.

Being held liable, and feeling that society deems us responsible, many of us parents believe we must *control* our teenagers . . . somehow.

And it's not just the legal system that pushes us in that direction. Don't you sometimes feel pressure—real or perceived—coming from other adults?

- "What will the teacher think if I don't get my son to speak up more in class?"
- "What will my sister think if my daughter doesn't send out thank-you notes for her birthday gift?"
- "What will the leaders think if my son's the only one at Scouts who hasn't had a shower?"

Do you feel "socially liable" for your teen's actions and attitudes—even when you're not really responsible? Does that feeling nudge you to control your son or daughter? This pressure can be a huge obstacle to healthy parenting—and sanity. Don't fall for it, and try not to subject other parents to it, either.

Being *responsible* means taking appropriate ownership of what is mine to be in charge of—in control of—and doing whatever needs to be done.

I have a 1987 Toyota 4Runner. I love it. It's *mine*. I *own* it. I also take *responsibility* for it. How? I pay the registration fee, put gas in the tank, see that it gets proper maintenance, and wash it. I'm acting *responsibly*. And in doing so, I also reap the benefits of having an awesome vehicle.

I am *not* responsible for *your* vehicle. Why not? Because it's not *mine*. I don't own it. I'm not in a position to "respond" to it.

Your vehicle belongs to you. You're responsible for it; I'm not. It's not that I *don't like* your vehicle. It's just not *mine*.

Getting on the Grid

So how does a parent mind his or her own business and still parent?

To answer that question, look at the following diagram. I call it the Control Grid.

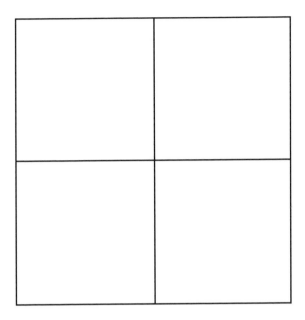

Looks pretty empty, doesn't it? Don't worry; it's not finished yet.

There are four boxes, or quadrants, in our diagram. Each quadrant represents a specific style of relating to or interacting with another person. These are not personality types (which are mostly unchangeable), but ways you—and your teenager—may *interact relationally* in any given situation.

A person can use any of the four styles. In fact, you may find yourself or your teenager bouncing back and forth among different styles during a single conversation about one topic.

Let's look at each style.

Style One: Hold

HOLD represents the interacting style that takes the "What I Can Control" category and says, "This is what I take responsibility for."

When you're a HOLDer, the following terms could be used to accurately describe you:
- responsible
- honest; truthful with yourself and others
- trustworthy; others can count on you to follow through with what you control
- willing to accept consequences; responding to things you can control, accepting the results of your actions
- taking ownership of yourself

The HOLDer says, "What's mine is mine." When you use this style, you hold on to the things that are legitimately yours to control and are therefore responsible for. You keep what's yours to keep. You're responsible for it.

Anybody using this style of relating will have confidence. I'm not talking about self-esteem; I mean a confidence in one's abilities and character. The more honest you are with yourself and with me, the more confident you'll be.

This is one of two healthy styles of interacting, whether you're the teenager or the parent.

Style Two: Toss

TOSSers take the "What I Can Control" category and say, "I don't take responsibility for it."

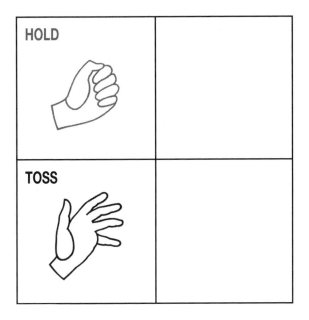

If you—or your teenager—are a TOSSer, the following terms could be used to describe you (or him or her):

- irresponsible
- liar, denier, blamer; pointing fingers at everybody else for your own actions
- avoider; not responding to what's yours

- untrustworthy
- shirking consequences any way you can

The TOSSer says, "What's mine is yours." When you use this style, you toss off your responsibilities. You try to unload your stuff onto somebody else, for him or her to handle, fix, be responsible for, and bear the consequences of.

This is the interactive style we often see in our teenagers. Does the following sound familiar? "It's not my fault, Mom. *You* didn't wake me up in time to study for my test this morning! And besides, it was an awful test anyway. The teacher should never have given it, especially on Monday morning! That's just stupid."

But before you think only teenagers are capable of TOSSing, think again.

"Son, you ruined my entire day. Can't you see you're making your mother have migraines? She can't help it if she worries about you. If you'd stop being such a jerk, maybe we could have some sanity in this house again."

It's easy for parents to be TOSSers as well.

Since confidence grows in direct proportion to honesty, and people using the TOSS style are not being honest, this style will erode confidence. Even if I get away with blaming somebody else and he or she takes the fall for my actions, I won't gain genuine assurance about my character and abilities.

This is *not* a healthy style to use. It won't help anybody.

Style Three: Grab

GRAB is the style that takes the "What I Can't Control" category and says, "I take responsibility for it."

For a GRABer, the following descriptions often would be accurate:

- overresponsible; trying to bear burdens that aren't really yours
- fixer, rescuer, enabler, codependent

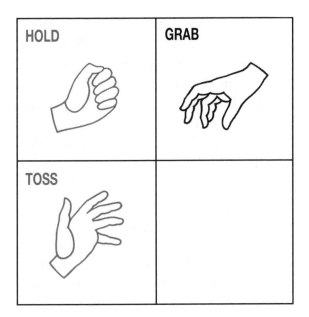

- martyr; an "Oh, poor me" person
- accepting consequences for wrongs you didn't even commit
- overcontrolling or intimidating
- taking ownership of yourself *and* others
- thinking problems are your fault: "If only I would . . ."
- manipulator; trying to force the outcome of a situation you have no legitimate control over

The GRABer says, "What's yours is mine." Maybe your teenager TOSSes and you GRAB what he or she just TOSSed. Sometimes you may start GRABing even before he or she starts TOSSing. "I'll just handle it all from the beginning," you think.

This is a style of interacting parents often find themselves in. They think,

If it's my fault as a parent, I can "fix" it because I'm a responsible person. If I can fix it, it will turn out the way I want it to.

But that's not reality. You don't control the way other people turn out. You're not God, so please don't try to play Him.

What happens to confidence when you use this style? You can't win the game of controlling the uncontrollable, and losing tends to destroy confidence. If it appears that you *did* win, you may gain a false sense of confidence. Either way, it's not a healthy relating style—no matter how spiritual we might try to make it sound. It's not healthy to take responsibility for things you can't control—nor is it based on truth.

Style Four: Fold

The FOLDer takes the "What I Can't Control" category and says, "I don't take responsibility for it." Think of FOLDing your hands in front of you—refusing to GRAB what isn't your problem.

| HOLD | GRAB |
| TOSS | FOLD |

When you're FOLDing, the following terms probably would describe you:

- minding your own business
- honest; letting others know what's yours and what's theirs
- trustworthy; can be counted on to keep your hands off what doesn't belong to you
- letting consequences fall where they belong (on the other person), even if it's hard to stand by and watch
- not taking ownership of the other person's stuff

FOLDers say, "What's yours is yours." We need to practice this style more often and teach our teenagers to do the same. It's the other healthy style of interaction.

Using this style of relating may give the appearance that you don't care, but that's not true. I do care about your car; it's just not my vehicle to wash.

Daily we're affected by things we have no control over. It's easy to fall into the trap of thinking, *Well, since it affects me, I should have some control over it!* In doing so, you slide up the diagram and end up interacting as a GRABer.

If it's not yours to own, keep your hands FOLDed. Don't take responsibility for it, even if it has a huge impact on you. That's life.

Remember Mark and Mandy and the fender bender? FOLD is the interactive style I encouraged Mark to use, even though he had to pay for repairing the other vehicle. He wasn't in control and wasn't responsible, though he was liable for the financial damages.

This style is harder to use than it may first appear. It's painful to be affected by something you don't have control over. It makes us feel "out of control"—because it *is* out of our control.

It's also hard to see someone you love—your teenager—"shoot himself in the foot" while keeping your hands FOLDed. When your son or daughter hurts, it hurts you, too. It's hard to be the one to press assault charges against your son. It's embarrassing to walk through the church lobby after spending Saturday night at the police station, bailing your daughter out of jail. It's hard to let our own flesh and blood make stupid mistakes that we know will shape them for the rest of their lives—sometimes in huge ways.

But the truth is still, "What's yours is yours, and what's theirs is theirs."

Remember to HOLD and FOLD. Those are the healthy styles of interacting. Avoid the TOSS and GRAB styles. Those are unhealthy ways of interacting with another person—especially your teenager.

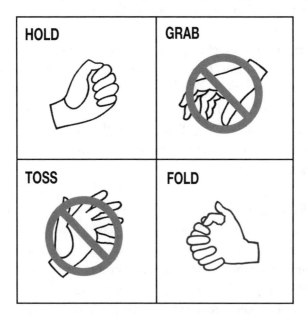

Keep Drawing Those Lines

Mark FOLDed his hands when it came to Mandy's auto accident—because it was hers, not his. What Mark did next, he did as a HOLDer. He took the copied key from Mandy (after determining that Mandy had only one made) and meted out a consequence.

If memory serves me correctly, this was the penalty: Mark took the door off Mandy's room for two weeks. More precisely, he took the door *he* owned off the room *he* owned, which Mandy was living in. The door was legitimately under his control.

But did he do this in order to control Mandy?

No. He was trying to *influence* Mandy with the consequence. It was Rule Three in action: "There's always somebody or something whose job is to make your life miserable when you choose stupid."

Your goal is to influence, not control, your teenager. I'll have more to say about that in Chapter 7. In the meantime, though, let's look at three habits that can keep us in the "control" rut and away from the influencing we really need to do.

SIX

Three Habits of Highly Controlling People

It's one thing to understand the difference between what you can control and what you can't. It's another to act on that understanding.

Why? Because many of us parents have some bad habits that keep elbowing us to grab control that doesn't belong to us. We may nod our heads at the Three Rules of Life and the Four Quadrants of the Control Grid, but certain ways of thinking keep tripping us up. We can be stuck in these habits and not realize it because our patterns are so ingrained.

In this chapter we'll examine three habits that can cause problems for even the most dedicated parent. They can be even more dangerous than your teen's most foolish behavior, driving you toward control that interferes with his or her growth and damages your relationship.

Habit One: "Should" Thinking

The first trap is that of perfectionistic thinking, otherwise known as "should" thinking. Before you dismiss the subject because you think you're not a perfectionist, read on.

Perfectionism is more subtle than having to have things "just so," and it's not revealed by the neatness of your closet or work area. It's based on how you think things *should* be. It holds a rigid view of how things *should* be done in order to be "right"—that there is one correct way to do something and you *should* do it *that* particular way.

Perfectionistic thinking falls along a continuum; it's not all or nothing. As you read this section, see if any of the patterns fit you or someone you know—a little, some, or a whole lot.

Do any of these statements sound familiar?

- "Zach, you *should* have studied more for your math test."
- "Amy *should* have known to call us first."
- "I *shouldn't* have yelled at Ryan that way."
- "Jason, you *shouldn't* argue with me, ever."
- "I *should* be grateful Emily's not in prison."
- "I *should* be a better parent."

The statements wrapped around a *should* or *shouldn't* may sound good—even biblical—but are inherently dangerous to your teenager and to you.

Take the example of Claire, a mom who worried about her 16-year-old daughter, Becca. The girl gravitated toward non-Christian guys instead of dating Christians. Claire thought Becca *should* marry a Christian, which meant she *should* date only Christians. Claire also believed Becca *should want* to date only Christians because the girl knew she *should*—not just because her mother thought she *should*.

Claire's attempt to control Becca's dating, thinking, and belief system led this mom to engage in manipulative tactics. She would tell every boy Becca brought home that her daughter "leads a Bible study" and "goes to church all the time." Claire would even ask the boys, "How did *you* become a Christian?" right in front of Becca.

The issue here isn't whether it's okay to marry outside the faith; Scripture says, "Do not be yoked together with unbelievers" (2 Corinthians 6:14). The issue is that "should" thinking took away Claire's power to influence Becca. Claire thought that if Becca didn't date the "right" way, the girl would turn out wrong and Claire would be a parental failure.

Not only did Claire's "should" thinking drive her nuts; the manipulative behaviors and statements drove Becca nuts, too. By "going for the bad guys," Becca was attempting to break her mother's hold, proving that Mom couldn't make her turn out "right."

"Should" statements are dangerous to you and your teenager for at least three reasons.

1. *The danger of condemning words.* Perfectionism tries to impose submission through condemnation—and the fear thereof. That's why a *should* statement is followed by a put-down, usually unspoken:

- "Zach, you *should* have studied more for your math test . . . but you didn't, Lazy!"
- "Amy, you *should* have known to call us first . . . but you didn't, Selfish!"
- "I *shouldn't* have yelled at Ryan that way . . . but I did, so I'm an idiot!"

Can you hear the condemnation? If you want your life to be riddled with criticism, that's your choice. But it's no way to be a healthy parent. Why condemn yourself or your teenager?

2. *The danger of giving up choices.* "Should" thinking leaves you and the other person with no viable options. You have to do things the "should" way or you're "wrong." You failed. You lost.

When you have no real choices, you have no real control. The power to influence has been snatched away from you—not by your teenager, but by your own unhealthy thinking pattern.

Living without choices is no way to parent. It's no fun living without the power to influence.

3. *The danger of preventing healthy pride.* When you do something well, "should" thinking keeps you from getting any credit for it. After all, that's how you *should* have done it in the first place.

Tim says, "Mom, I got an A on my calculus test!"

Mom replies, "Well, Tim, you had to take it five times. You *should* get an A on it by now."

Clunk. That's the sound of a lead balloon hitting the floor.

Where's Mom's excitement for me? Where is rejoicing "with those who rejoice" (Romans 12:15)? That's what "should" thinking does for you and your teenager.

Because control often feels more powerful and certain than influence does, many of us parents resort to "should" thinking in an effort to control ourselves and our teens. "Should" thinking also leads us to do things not by choice, but out of obligation and fear of condemnation.

Breaking Habit One

To overcome perfectionist patterns, we need to question our "shoulds" and our right to enforce them.

So who made you God? How did you come to know it all and have the power to pick the one "right" way to do everything?

I don't mean to be disrespectful toward you or toward God. I'm asking sincerely whether you have the right to decide what *should* and *shouldn't* be.

Most of us want to be the decision-maker. Some of us even tag God's name on our decision so it sounds spiritual and more "right."

But even if a principle is straight out of Scripture, God has never *forced* people into obedience or turned human beings into robots. Remember how He treated Adam and Eve; He let them choose.

Later, through Joshua, God told the nation of Israel, "*Choose for yourselves* this day whom you will serve, whether the gods your forefathers served beyond the River, or the gods of the Amorites, in whose land you are living" (Joshua 24:15, italics added).

Israel *could* choose the gods of its forefathers beyond the river.

Israel *could* choose the gods of the Amorites.

Israel *could* choose the Lord.

There was no "You have to . . ." or "You should . . ."

Joshua finished his presentation in that verse with a resounding, unashamed, freely made choice. He said, "But as for me and my household, we will serve the LORD."

So how do you give up the "shoulds" and give your teenager a choice?

Again, let me generalize Jesus' statement, "You will know the truth, and the truth will set you free" (John 8:32). "Should" thinking can be changed for the better. It's a matter of exchanging a lie for the truth—even if that lie has been in our mental jukebox for decades.

The lie: "I *should* pray for my kids every morning."

The truth: "I *could* . . . I *would like to* . . . I *choose to* pray for my kids every morning, or as many mornings as I can."

Before you think I'm simply playing a psychological word game, check it out. Which statement is actually more truthful? Where is it written that on this planet, in this millennium, on this continent, that this person (you) should pray for your kids every day?

There isn't a law that says that, which means you didn't break any law. Which means you didn't do anything wrong.

Now, is the statement "I *would like to* pray for my kids every morning" true?

In my case it is. I really do *want* to pray for them every morning if possible. And so I *choose* freely and willingly to engage in prayer on their behalf.

Could . . .

Would like . . .

I wish . . .

I choose . . .

These are the antidotes to "should" thinking.

Let's say I'm disappointed that I didn't pray for my kids this morning. I'm sad, but I'm not condemned. I'm not a failure because I came up short against a *should* statement that's only in my head. Yes, I will continue to work on being more faithful with my morning prayers, disciplining myself to get to bed earlier so I can be awake in the morning. I'm reaching for what I *want*, and that won't stop. But there is no condemnation.

Almost sounds biblical, doesn't it? "There is now no condemnation for those who are in Christ Jesus" (Romans 8:1).

"So how do I change my thinking patterns?"

Glad you asked. Here's an exercise that has worked for me and for some of my clients. I call it "Let's Make a Deal."

Pretend that you have a son who, like Zach in the earlier example, "should" have studied more for a math test.

Step 1: On a piece of paper, write the words "should" and "shouldn't" in bold letters. Below those words, write, "My son *should* have studied more for that math test."

On another sheet of paper, write the words "could," "I wish," and "I choose" in bold letters. Below these words, rewrite the sentence using one of the words or phrases on this sheet. Examples: "My son *could* have studied more for that math test." "*I wish* he had studied more for that math test." "*I choose* to remind him to study for his math test next time I know one's coming."

Step 2: Lay both pieces of paper in front of you, faceup.

Step 3: Decide which set of words—which thinking pattern—you want to keep and live by.

Step 4: Whichever piece of paper you choose to live by, keep. Destroy the other one.

If you choose to keep the "could" paper, next comes the hard work. Every time you have an opportunity to use "should" or "shouldn't," stop yourself. Use one of the other options. Do this when you talk with your teenager—and to replace some of those recordings in your mental jukebox.

It will take conscious effort, especially at first, but will be worth it in the end. Dropping the "should" habit may take anywhere from a few weeks to several months, so be patient with yourself and keep working. This is one way to "be transformed by the renewing of your mind" (Romans 12:2).

This exercise changed a family I know. I was counseling the mom and dad, both seasoned experts at beating themselves and others up with "should" thinking. After we used the exercise, they accused me of taking away half their vocabulary! In the end, though, they thanked me—feeling less condemned by their own thinking and by each other. The atmosphere in their house finally felt free; their teenage son noticed how much more "peaceful" it seemed. The entire family learned to speak and think the "could" way. The husband said, "It's made a huge difference throughout our whole house!"

Habit Two: "What If" Thinking

The second bad habit that encourages control-grabbing involves another thinking pattern: worry. Some basic definitions are critical.

- fear: an intense emotional reaction to a *legitimate, present* danger
- anxiety: an intense emotional reaction, usually of dread, to a *perceived, anticipated,* or *future* danger
- worry: the nontechnical term for anxiety
- concern: the Christianized version of anxiety; since we know we *shouldn't* worry, we change it to being "concerned," even though a horse by any other color is still a horse
- panic: an ill-advised behavioral reaction to being overwhelmed by fear or anxiety
- obsession: a persistent, often unwanted flooding of thoughts that is very difficult to stop
- obsessive-compulsive disorder: a condition in which you attempt to stop obsessive thinking by engaging in repetitive behavior such as hand washing, counting, double-checking, cleaning, and reciting words or phrases over and over

Anxiety shows itself in many ways. Here's a partial list of how it can be displayed:

- trembling or shaking
- excessive worrying
- restlessness, being "keyed-up" or "on edge"
- being easily fatigued
- having difficulty concentrating
- sleep problems
- always having a "Plan A," "Plan B," and more
- avoiding situations or decisions you're unsure about
- feeling stuck and unable to make decisions without much effort
- fear of being wrong
- thinking, always thinking
- having to know what's going to happen next
- having a feeling of impending failure or rejection
- being overcontrolling
- feeling out of control
- depression
- anger, often for no apparent reason

I'm not going to focus on clinical anxiety, but more on the "street anxiety" we all know and call worry. Like perfectionism, it's more a thinking pattern than a behavior. The pattern can be summed up in the phrase, "What if?"

"*What if* Jeremy ends up in jail?"

"*What if* Susan doesn't get that college scholarship?"

"*What if* we were too hard on Kenny and he runs away again?"

Try listing your own "what ifs" regarding your parenting or your teenager.

The problem with "*what if*" thinking is your focus. Anxiety pulls you into the future and away from the present.

Present-tense fear says, "The house is burning now. Run!"

Worry, on the other hand, says, "*What if* the house starts to burn tonight when we're all sleeping?" Many of the things we worry about never come to pass.

To make this more concrete, let's take an example that involves rock climbing, an activity I enjoy. Let's say I've invited your son to go climbing at Garden of the Gods in Colorado Springs; you've decided to come along and watch.

As your son is climbing, you don't worry about the going-up part. It's the possible falling-down part that bothers you.

But is that falling in the *past*, the *present*, or the *future*?

"The past."

No. He may have fallen in the past, and you remember how much he got skinned up and you don't want him to do that again. But you're not really fretting about the past. You're worried that he *may* fall in the *future*. His body is in the present, climbing and having a grand old time. But your mind gets sucked into the black hole of the future "what if" world.

"*What if* he falls?"

"*What if* his hand slips off the hold?"

The future doesn't exist yet. What control do you have over things that don't exist?

None. So you feel out of control—even though he's going up, not down.

Now, let's say your son does slip and is falling. You're not worried about his falling now; you're dreading his hitting the ground.

Is that impact in the past, present, or future?

"The future."

Right. It's less than three seconds in the future, but it's still the future. Knowing what kind of stop it will be hasn't happened yet.

Moments later, he's stopped. *Now* what are you worried about?

"*What if* he's really hurt?"

"*What if* he's permanently injured?"

"*What if* it's my fault because I let him go climbing with Tim in the first place?"

"*What if* he misses work on Monday and his boss decides to fire him?"

"*What if* my wife yells at me for this?"

When we worry, our minds move into the "what if" world of the future. It's understandable, but makes as much sense as trying to find out what happens next in a movie you're watching so you can be ready for it. You run into the projection booth and try to watch the movie 24 frames ahead of the lamp. It doesn't work.

I once got a call from a mother complaining about her daughter. The daughter wouldn't help around the house, wouldn't get a job, and was constantly belligerent and disrespectful. Whenever the caller attempted to confront the daughter, the latter would yell, blame her "uncaring" mother for any problems, and even threaten suicide.

Imagine the "what if" thinking in this mother's head:

"*What if* it really is my fault?"

"*What if* she never believes me when I tell her I care about her?"

"*What if* she does commit suicide?"

Believe it or not, the "child" in this story was 41 years old! The mother was still trying to "mother" her adult daughter, still trying to rescue and fix her daughter using the GRAB style of relating. Worrying made this mother powerless.

You may think worry keeps you in control, because you'll be "ready" for whatever comes. Or you may think your worries justify attempts to snatch control that isn't yours. But neither is true.

Breaking Habit Two

"How can I stop the worry thinking?"

Hang in there. With a little help, you can change. Be patient with yourself.

I speak from experience, because I'm a recovering perfectionist and worrier—if there is such a thing. When I became aware of the "what if" thinking running through my mind from morning until late at night, I began to ask around for ideas to stop it. What I got was loosely based on Bible verses:

"Just don't worry about tomorrow" (Matthew 6:34).

"Take every thought captive" (2 Corinthians 10:5).

"Just think about good things" (Philippians 4:8).

I would always respond by asking, "How?" All I got back were blank looks. Nobody could tell me how to shut down the thinking pattern in my head.

So I tried to find some answers on my own. I discovered that breaking the "what if" habit is similar to breaking the "should" habit. First, identify the "what ifs" ricocheting off the inside of the jukebox of your mind. Next, stop that record and replace it with the thinking pattern you *want* to have.

To help myself in this brain transition, I pieced together the following four-question technique. It seems rather silly, but it works. I've been teaching it to anxiety-prone clients for many years now, and it's helped a lot of them.

Write the following four questions on an index card:

1. What are five colors I see right now?
2. What are five sounds I hear right now (even if I have to make them, like scratching on the chair armrest)?
3. What are five things I physically feel (not emotions, but things like "my watch on my wrist" or "wind in my hair")?
4. What do I need to be doing—or thinking about—*right now?*

Since worrying is a bad thinking habit, you need to get the warped record out of your jukebox by creating a new habit, a new record. Habits are built on repetition, so place the card on your nightstand or dresser. When you wake up, go over the four questions to get your brain going in a new direction first thing in the morning. Ask and answer the questions yourself, out loud if possible.

After naming those five colors, five sounds, and five things you physically feel, ask yourself what you need to do when your feet hit the floor. Go to the bathroom? Put your robe on and go make some coffee?

Don't try to handle the whole rest of the day right now. It's not here in the present; it's in the future. Don't get sucked into "what if" thinking about the day, *just make the coffee.*

You see, moments are like snowflakes. One snowflake looks pretty; a billion of them equal a blizzard. You *can* handle this moment. What you *can't* handle is all the unknown snowflakes of the future combined. It's a blizzard in your brain.

This doesn't mean you don't make plans. Making plans happens in the *present.* The problem is trying to live in the future.

Take your index card, or a copy of it, with you and review the four questions three to five times a day. Ask them again as you get ready for bed at night. If it's Wednesday night, don't worry about Thursday or Friday. Stay in Wednesday. Enjoy going to bed instead of fretting about whether you'll be rested up for that important meeting tomorrow. One snowflake at a time.

When I began using this technique myself, I had no idea if it would work. I just knew I had to do something different from what I'd been doing all those years. I had to find a way to slow down the worry that was driving me "out of control."

But in the course of two to three months, the change happened. The present began to take root, and the "what if" records played less and less. That thinking still sneaks in sometimes, but not nearly as often. Now that I'm more focused on *what is,* the "what if" feels foreign.

The same can happen for you.

Habit Three: Living in the Past

A third control-oriented trap is often labeled by therapists as "living one generation back." To see if you tend to do this, consider the following statements. Have you ever made them or others like them?

- "I'll never be gone as much as my father was."
- "I resent my mother. She was too strict. She suffocated my brother and me and still tries to today, if I let her. I'm never going to try to run my kids' lives."
- "I never got to play baseball because the games were always on Sunday, and Dad didn't believe in 'working on the Lord's Day.' When I have kids, I'm gonna be sure they get a chance to play baseball, even if all the games are on Sunday."

Those attitudes and decisions are prompted by people who are living in the past. All these parents are trying to undo old hurts through the lives of their children today.

Most of the time parents do this unknowingly, unintentionally. But in the end, it's selfish to use your children for your own gain. And it leads some parents to grab control in order to make sure the gain happens.

How harmful is this pattern? It can create the opposite result of the outcome the parent wants.

A dad I knew, Andy, is a perfect example. Andy's dream was to play professional baseball. His only goal in life was to pitch for a major league team. Because of a rotator cuff injury that wouldn't heal correctly, that dream was unrealized.

So what's a guy to do? Andy began pushing his son, Brandon, into baseball, and pressured him into pitching.

Brandon was a normal boy who wanted to please his father. So he followed his father's lead. It was easy because Brandon was naturally athletic, just like his dad, and he liked baseball.

But Andy couldn't let Brandon just enjoy the game, because Brandon *had* to make it to the majors. He *had* to live out his father's dream in his father's place. This eventually blew up in Andy's face when Brandon lost his love for the game and chose not to even finish out his college years in a uniform.

Breaking Habit Three

It's wise to learn from the past. Just don't try to "fix" it vicariously through your teenager's life now.

We all have hopes, dreams, expectations, and desires for our kids. That's normal and healthy. But those dreams and expectations can become a trap when you hold them too tightly and attempt to squeeze reality—in the form of your son or daughter—into them.

Dreams for your teenager are fine. Objectives for healthy behavior and living are good and necessary. But be careful about placing expectations on your teenager that are really for yourself. Be careful about making goals out of things you can't accomplish by your own effort.

Don't live one generation back. Don't parent there, either.

Creature of Habit?

Do any of these habits sound familiar? If they don't fit you, might they fit your spouse? If so, be careful to take the beam out of your own eye before trying to help your spouse with the speck in his or hers.

If you find any of these thinking patterns in your life, I'd encourage you to spend more time here—or come back to this chapter once you finish the book. Work on the habits that apply to you. Staying out of these traps can make "losing control" of your teen a less daunting task.

If you've already recognized these tendencies in your thinking and have been working on them, keep at it. Be patient with yourself and give credit where it's due.

If you don't find yourself falling into any of these traps, great! That's one less thing to worry about, right?

PART III

Turning Off the Power Struggle

SEVEN

Dances of Influence

The purpose of this book is to help you see the difference between *control* and *influence*. Even if we parents don't have control over our teenagers' thoughts or behaviors, that doesn't mean we lack *influencing* power over our teens and each specific circumstance.

So now comes the moment you've been waiting for. What is *influence* and how does it work?

As a verb, the word *influence* means to affect, impress, move, bias, incline, sway, inspire, infiltrate, or "pull strings." Influence can be overt or covert, subtle or blatant, mild or wild. It can be very powerful—and *influential.*

Believe it or not, you as a parent can have a tremendous influence on your teenager. Exercising that power wisely is part of your responsibility. *Influencing* while losing *control* is a bit like walking a tightrope strung across a deep gorge . . . with a strong side wind!

When you influence, all your persuading and inspiring still allows the other person to make the final choice. That person keeps the control. He or she is responsible for his or her actions, thoughts, and feelings.

Yes, you encourage the person to see things your way. You may try to talk her out of doing some stupid thing she's contemplating.

But in all your attempts to inspire, sway, motivate, and infiltrate your teenager's thought process—which parents need never feel ashamed of—you don't try to force his thinking or behavior by coercing or manipulating. You let him choose and retain the control that's rightfully his.

"So," you ask, "if I take the car keys away from my 18-year-old son, am I trying to control him or influence him?"

That's a great question. The answer is not in the taking of the keys, but in your motive for taking them. One way to tell whether you're trying to control or influence is to figure out what kind of relational "dance" you're doing with your teen.

Shall We Dance?

Remember the Control Grid from Chapter 5? Using its four styles of interacting (HOLD, GRAB, TOSS, and FOLD), there are four possible dances that can occur when two people interact. This is true with any two human beings, and in any setting—at work, church, the grocery store, or a family reunion. Whenever two humans attempt to interact, you'll find one of these four dances.

Let's look at these dances, using four versions of a teen-parent situation I've encountered in my counseling. Of course, I've made some changes in the actual dialogue and added some hypothetical elements. Consider the roles of control and influence in each dance.

Dance One: the HOLD and GRAB

In this example the teen is a HOLDer. Remember, that's the type who takes responsibility for what he can control. He says, "What's mine is mine."

But the parent here is a GRABer. She tries to take responsibility for things she can't control. She says, "What's yours is mine."

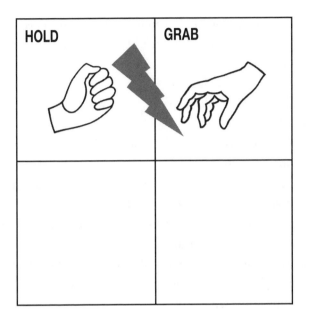

I'll play the part of the 16-year-old son and use my name in the story.

TIM: "That's so dumb! I can't believe I flunked the written part of my driver's test. Man, I can ace the driving part! I guess I didn't study enough."

(Notice how I'm taking ownership of my failed test.)

MOM: "Honey, I'm so sorry you didn't pass the test. Come here. I'll make you your favorite brownies. I'm sorry I didn't help you enough; I've just been stressed out with your dad traveling so much lately. I guess I should have helped you study more. I'm sorry. I didn't even think about giving you the sample test I saw on the Internet last week. Go get the book and I'll study it with you."

(Mom is GRABing, trying to control the outcome by taking ownership and blame. It's not the same as validating my feelings and helping me take ownership. She's not trying to influence me, she's trying to fix something that isn't hers to fix.)

TIM: "It's okay, Mom. I can handle it. I'm just frustrated, that's all."

MOM: "No, I'm sorry I haven't been more involved in your life lately. Let me help you."

TIM: "Mom, I'll be okay."

MOM: "I said I would help you, and I will."

TIM: "But, Mom—"

MOM: "No 'buts.' Go get the manual. I'll quiz you right now on the questions you missed."

This dance happens a lot more than you might expect. We may not notice it because the teenager's plan for "fixing" things may seem unwise or incomplete. Still, even if you're trying to "help," that's no reason to reach for the responsibility yourself.

This dance produces tension and strain. Why? Because both participants are trying to control the same thing. And two people can't own the same thing at the same time.

In this case, the teenager is using a healthy style of interacting. The parent isn't. The teen is trying to HOLD on to control that belongs to him, and Mom is trying to take it away. Get ready for a fight, because teenagers don't want to be controlled or manipulated—directly or covertly.

Mom needs to take her hands off and let Tim learn on his own. She can influence what he does next, but her stab at control won't help either of them.

Dance Two: the TOSS and GRAB

In this example the teen is a TOSSer. Remember, that's the type who refuses responsibility for what he can control. He says, "What's mine is yours."

The parent here is a GRABer, as in Dance One.

TIM: "That's so stupid! I can't believe I flunked the written part of the driver's test. Man, I can ace the driving part! Mom, why didn't you make me study that stupid manual more?"

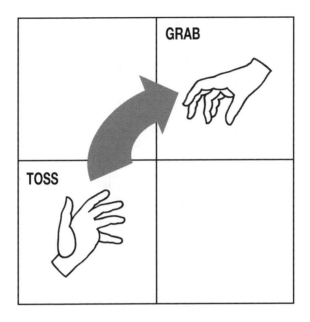

(Notice how I'm trying to push ownership of my failed test onto Mom, expecting her to take the blame and fix the problem.)

MOM: "Honey, I'm so sorry you didn't pass the test. Come here. I'll make you your favorite brownies. I'm sorry I didn't help you enough; I've just been stressed out with your dad traveling so much lately. I guess I should have helped you study more. I'm sorry. I didn't even think about giving you the sample test I saw on the Internet last week. Here, go get the book and I'll study with you. I'll also call the DMV to see if I can make arrangements to retake the test without having to pay for it. Okay?"

(Mom is GRABing again.)

TIM: "Where'd you put the book, anyway?"

MOM: "I don't know. What did you do with it?"

TIM: "How should I know? You're the one who's always going around and cleaning up my stuff—putting it where I can never find it again."

MOM: "I'll look for it as soon as I finish paying these bills."

TIM: "Whatever."

Does this sound familiar? It's far more common than Dance One, especially in homes with a teenager. The terrible thing about this dance is that it "works." The teenager TOSSes; the parent GRABs. There's no real tension. It's like you're playing a game of catch.

One problem with this dance is that the TOSSing goes in only one direction—away from the teen and toward the parent. It's not a healthy way to interact. Another problem is that the parent isn't influencing; she's still trying to control the outcome by GRABing. The teen's TOSSing seems to invite this, but that doesn't mean it's a good idea for either party.

When a parent dances this way, it's often because this recording is playing in his or her jukebox: *If it's my fault, then I can fix it. If I can fix it, it will turn out the way I want it to.* The parent is trying to control a part of the world he or she can't control.

The lack of tension in the "TOSS and GRAB" dance fools some parents and teens into thinking all is well on the Western Front. It fools some parents into thinking they're acting responsibly. It also gives teens a false sense of power—and parents a false sense of being needed.

Dance Three: the TOSS and FOLD

This time the teen is once again a TOSSer, declining to take responsibility for what he can control.

But the parent is a FOLDer. She doesn't take responsibility for things she can't control. She says, "What's yours is yours."

TIM: "That's so stupid! I can't believe I flunked the written part of the driver's test. Man, I can ace the driving part! Mom, why didn't you make me study that stupid manual more?"

(I'm still TOSSing.)

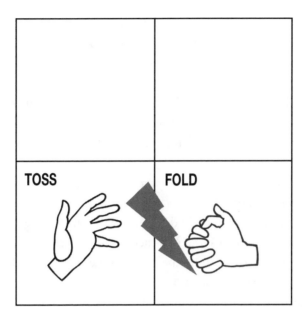

MOM: "Honey, I'm so sorry you didn't pass your test. Come here. I'll make you your favorite brownies."

(Did you notice the new pronoun? "You didn't pass your test." It's subtle, but makes all the difference.)

MOM: "I'm sorry you flunked your driving test. What do you think you need to do to ace it next time you take it? I saw a sample test on the Internet last week. If you want the Web site, just let me know. Maybe it will help you get ready to take it again soon."

(Mom's hands are FOLDed. She's not accepting responsibility, not GRABing for control. She's sympathetic, but not taking the blame.)

TIM: "It's not my fault. You didn't make me study!"

MOM: "No, Tim. It's not my fault. I passed my driver's test a long time ago. This is your license to earn, not mine."

TIM: "Don't you *want* me to get my driver's license? You don't care about me, do you?"

(Yes, the FOLD style can be misinterpreted as "I don't care." But Mom is simply refusing to engage in a power struggle. She's making sure I keep my own control by not GRABing for it, and letting me HOLD the consequences of my own foolish choice.)

MOM: "Tim, Dad and I *do* care about you. This is something that's not ours to be responsible for. Whether you pass your driver's test is up to you. You may want to plan to study so you'll be ready for it next time."

(Mom's not trying to fix it because it's not hers to fix. She's trying to influence me by giving me good advice about studying more.)

When you're caught up in this dance with your teenager, hold your ground! You're doing it right! Yes, there's tension—but that's not your fault. The tension comes from the TOSSer's use of an unhealthy style of interacting, and you're not letting him get away with it.

Sure, this dance can be tiring. But if you keep holding your ground, one of two things will happen:

1. The tension will continue. That's a bummer, but don't cave in.

2. Your teenager will eventually move up the grid, start being a HOLDer, and take responsibility for what he can control. Good for you! You may even have influenced him to choose smart.

If you give in and GRAB just to relieve the tension, you've gone back to the TOSS and GRAB dance. Don't do that. Hang in there.

Dance Four: the HOLD and FOLD

In this case the teen is a HOLDer. He takes responsibility for what he can control. That's a good thing.

The parent is a FOLDer. She doesn't take responsibility for what she can't control. That's a good thing, too.

TIM: "That's so dumb! I can't believe I flunked the written part of my driver's test. Man, I can ace the driving part! I guess I didn't study enough."

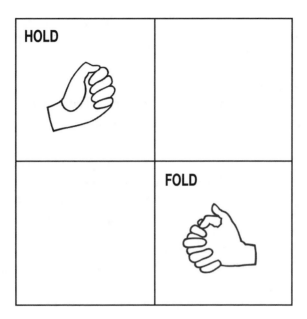

(I'm owning the problem.)

MOM: "Honey, I'm so sorry you didn't pass your test. Come here. I'll make you your favorite brownies. What do you think you need to do to pass it next time? I did notice a sample test on the Internet last week. If you want the Web site, just let me know. Maybe that will help you get ready to take it again soon."

(Mom's FOLDing, letting me be. She's not taking it upon herself to ensure that I pass next time. She's trying to influence me, but not control.)

TIM: "Thanks, Mom. Let me know when the brownies are ready. I'm going to look for my manual. Any idea where it is?"

(I'm not trying to TOSS. Even if I don't do it very well, I want Mom to let me HOLD what I can control.)

MOM: "No, I don't know where your manual is. Did you look behind your desk? Things tend to fall behind there, you know."

(Mom is letting me live with the consequences of my behavior. She offers a good suggestion—to influence me, not to control the outcome.)

TIM: "I don't think it's back there, but I'll start there. If I don't find it, I guess I'll have to get another manual from the DMV office. This is so stupid."

MOM: "I hope you find it, honey."

In this dance, there's no battle or tension. The teen takes responsibility for his actions, and the parent lets him keep it. It's as simple as that.

That doesn't mean there's no impact on you—especially if you're the one who ends up driving the teen back to the Department of Motor Vehicles to get another copy of the driver's manual. But the license isn't yours to get. You're letting the teen experience the realities of life in attempting to get it.

If this dance unfolds in your home, you're doing it correctly! Keep it up.

Yes, it's a lot easier to FOLD when your teenager decides to HOLD. But you still get credit for FOLDing. If your teen tries to HOLD but isn't doing a very good job of it, keep FOLDing. Come alongside him or her and model how to HOLD more wisely. That's influence. Avoid the temptation to slide up the Control Grid and GRAB.

A Parent of Influence

So, is it *control* or *influence* to take away your 18-year-old's car keys?

Assuming it's not a situation in which your teen isn't able to exercise control (he or she is drunk, for instance), it depends on whether you're making a preemptive strike that eliminates your teen's options. Are you GRABing his or her power to pick smart or stupid? Or are you influencing by letting him or her experience the "ouch" of a poor choice already made (FOLDing)?

While you're at it, here are some other questions to ask yourself:

• Which of the four dances is most common in your home?

- On a scale of 1 to 10 (10 highest), what's the tension level when you and your teenager "dance"?

If there's tension in the relationship, chances are that someone isn't using a healthy style of interacting. It's either your teenager . . . or it's you.

Be sure it's not you. If it is, do what it takes to get yourself out of the GRAB or TOSS pattern. Talk with a friend, pastor, or counselor if you need to.

If you're HOLDing and FOLDing, stand your ground. Keep influencing, even when GRABing and TOSSing look easier. It's the healthiest way to "lose control" of your teen.

EIGHT

Rules of Engagement

- If you're mean to your sibling, you have to be his or her servant for an hour.
- If you're late for dinner, you lose video game time for the rest of the night.
- No country music can be played around Mom. (Rap is okay, but no country.)
- Everyone gets his or her own drink for dinner.
- No reading at the table if the whole family is there.
- No going on the roof to sit, sing, read, or whatever.
- No sliding down the stairs in cardboard boxes (though using a sleeping bag is fine).
- No prank phone calls.
- You're allowed only one mug of noodles per day.
- You can't eat the juice concentrate out of the can with a spoon.
- Don't pick off the turkey skin before the turkey is sliced and served.
- You may not stare at or bug the crazy woman who lives next door and sleeps in her front yard because she's afraid someone is going to come into her house and get her.

- iPods in the car may only be run through the speakers.
- If you're wearing braces, no orange brackets with the "Cheetos look."
- No underwear showing.
- No singing at the dinner table.

These are real household rules from real families. All of them make sense to someone—or did at one time. Some rules live on long after their initial purpose is forgotten—like that last family's no-singing-at-the-dinner-table rule.

Setting rules for your teenager can resemble trying to rid yourself of a hornet's nest using a three-foot shovel: It's awkward and full of surprises, not all of them pleasant. The subject of rules is complicated by the fact that they're often made in reaction to specific, unfortunate events. In the heat of the moment, parents step in and issue a decree "so it won't ever happen again."

There will always be rules. Workplaces, roads, schools, stores, sports—they all have rules. I'm sure heaven and hell will have them, too. Call me old-fashioned, but I support the idea that "if it's your house, it's your rules." That's life.

But when we try to use rules to control our teenagers' future behavior, we're on shaky ground. Rules can't really control anybody. It's pointless and counterproductive to try to control a teenager's developing belief system, attitudes, and the actions that flow from them.

Many parents, even if they know rules don't control people, use rules to keep their anxiety in check. *If Hannah is in bed by 9 P.M., then I won't have to worry about what she's up to.* If you're worrying in this way, please revisit the section on "what if" thinking in Chapter 6. Anxiety is *your* problem; don't make it your teenager's.

But does this mean you won't have rules? Not at all. It means understanding the purpose of rules, and the differences between rules, advice, and suggestions.

The Reasons for Rules

Let's consider the Garden of Eden again. In this perfect place with perfect children and a perfect parent, there was a rule.

It was, "You must not eat from the tree of the knowledge of good and evil" (Genesis 2:17). It wasn't, "You *shouldn't* eat of that tree," or "Stay away from dangerous fruit." It was a simple, clear command not to eat from a specific tree.

Why was there a rule in the Garden? The answer lies in the two reasons for any rule:

1. To keep safety in.
2. To keep chaos (un-safety) out.

That's as complicated as it gets. That's it.

Since you probably don't have a dictionary with you, let me review what safety and chaos mean.

Safety is being protected from damage or danger—physical, emotional, and spiritual.

The "damage" part of that definition is important. There are two kinds of hurt—the kind that causes actual damage and the kind that doesn't. Parents often get them mixed up.

When I go mountain bike riding with my buddies, I feel pain. My lungs start to burn (which happens when you ride hard at an altitude of over 9,000 feet). After a couple of hours my legs hurt. But when we stop and rest our feet on the side of the truck, the pain subsides; there's no damage done to my body parts.

The other kind of pain results from actual damage. In a fairly minor fall on my mountain bike, I broke a bone in my right hand. Not realizing it was broken, I kept riding. The pain got worse as I tried to shift and brake. The broken bone was doing more damage to the surrounding tissue. This is the kind of hurt that safety is protecting us from.

In our attempt to be responsible parents, we sometimes think our job is to protect our children from *all* pain—both kinds. But the first kind of pain is part of living and growing up. It's the second kind, the type that produces damage, that we're striving to protect our children from.

Chaos is a place or circumstance of confusion or disorder. Safety is compromised here, and the "damage" kind of pain is likely to happen.

With those definitions behind us, let's look at the rule in Genesis. Why did God put that tree off-limits? Because "you will surely die" (2:17). That's definitely a safety issue. It's all about damage.

Rules aren't for modifying behavior, instilling values, or changing attitudes. Here's where parents often go astray, writing regulations that attempt to do exactly these things.

It doesn't work. If you want to influence behavior or instill values or work on attitudes, you'll model, mentor, teach, and pray—over and over again. Remember that nothing will "make" your teenager change, and it's not your job to "make sure" he or she turns out "right."

The Three Rules of Life shed some light on this. Let's review them.

Rule One: Your teenager will live or die by his or her own choices. You can't control him or her, even with well-written rules.

Rule Two: Your teenager has the right to choose stupid or smart. That's true even if you've instituted all sorts of good rules.

Rule Three: It's your job to make your teenager's life a little miserable when he or she chooses stupid. When rules are broken, here's where dishing out consequences comes into play.

One of the roads between my house and office is Academy Boulevard. Every day I drive past a sign that reads, "Speed Limit 40." There is no sign saying, "You *should* go 40," or "Please, *please*, go 40." The rule is clearly stated—no more, no less.

Does that sign "make" me go the speed that's posted?

No.

Does that flat piece of metal "control" me in any way?

No.

Why?

Because I live or die by my own choices, not by signs. I also have the right to choose smart (go the posted speed) or stupid (exceed the posted limit). The rule doesn't control me at all.

So why the speed limit sign? To keep safety in . . . and chaos out.

Someone at the Colorado Springs Department of Transportation decided, after much research, that 40 miles per hour was a speed at which traffic could *safely* travel on that stretch of road. The limit increases the chances of keeping safety in and chaos out.

Rules don't control, just as a sign can't control a driver. They have consequences attached to them, though; breaking them can result in a $100 traffic ticket.

Rules, Advice, and Suggestions: What's the Difference?

Rule: "Be in bed by 10 P.M. The consequence if you break this rule is losing your allowance for the week."

Advice: "Be in bed by 10 P.M., or you'll be too tired to do well on your test tomorrow."

Suggestion: "Did you know it's already 10:00? You might want to go to bed before it gets any later."

We give advice to influence our teenagers' choices and the ways in which they think. We do it because we *want* them to act and think wisely. Advice is wise counsel. Advice is *influence*—an attempt to sway, persuade, and encourage your teenager in a particular direction.

Advice is not a law that exacts a penalty if "broken." If wise advice is ignored, natural consequences may follow. This is Rule Three in action.

Most parents, having been "around the block" a few more times than teenagers, have accumulated some wise counsel to share. So why do so many moms and dads choose to set down rules rather than give advice? Because advice doesn't have the same "bite" that rules have.

Advice seems too weak to have any real impact on a teenager. It's not true, but *feels* true to many parents.

Suggestions seem even less powerful. They're simply good ideas for positive choices. A suggestion doesn't define the way life *has* to be or what the only wise decision is. It just reflects a good idea or one smart way to do something.

Suggestions are given in an attempt to assist by sharing "common sense" you've learned. They're another form of influence.

Parents, of course, can fall into the trap of making "suggestions" to their teenagers that really aren't suggestions. They're "do-it-this-way" commands, disguised to sound "nice." If you're making a suggestion, your teenager is free to take it or leave it—without any consequence if it's "left."

Does this interchange between a mother and her teenage son, Jack, sound familiar?

"Jack, do you want to take the trash out to the Dumpster right now? It's full."

"No, I'll get it later."

"Jack, you come down here right now and take out this trash like I told you!"

Was Jack's mom "suggesting" Jack take out the trash? Was she really asking if he *wanted* to?

Jack answered with respect and honesty. He didn't *want* to, at least right now. So what's there to be so upset about? Was this a suggestion, or was it really a "do it now" statement?

Don't hide rules or commands in "suggestive" verbiage. Your teenager will likely take you literally and ignore your "hint"—especially if it's to his or her advantage!

Make sure rules are understood as rules, advice is understood as advice, and suggestions are understood as suggestions—especially by *you*. Often parents aren't clear in their own minds about which are which. These parents throw whatever they want into the "rule" category when they're trying to control their teenagers' present or future behavior.

Seven Principles of Writing Rules

I won't call these the rules of rule-writing. Let's call them key principles that can help you avoid common problems in this area.

1. *Have as few rules as possible.* You'll have to keep track of every rule you make. If you can't remember 19,324 house rules, don't expect your teenager to do it. Since consistency is an important ingredient of parenting, you'll have to make sure the rules are enforced every time they're broken. Do you want to spend your life being the house law enforcement officer?

Somebody has to do it, after all. Rules without consequences are meaningless and encourage teenagers not to believe you. Do you expect your teenager to tell you every time he's broken a rule and to request the appropriate consequence? Whenever a rule is broken, you'll have to confront your teenager as you enforce it.

The more rules you make, the more time you'll spend on the law-enforcement side of parenting. Being a parent *does* involve making and upholding rules. But if you spend too much time on that, you'll have less time for all the other responsibilities being a mom or dad entails. Is that a wise use of your precious time?

2. *Make the rule specific and quantitative.* The vaguer the rule, the more room there is for your teenager to wiggle out. Kids are good at that. Parents often *like* rules to be nebulous, so they can mold regulations into whatever form suits them at the moment.

Having specific, measurable rules keeps you in line, too. It forces you to be clear and purposeful about your real meanings and desires. It also helps keep manipulative tendencies in check.

3. *Make sure you can enforce the rule.* Rules you don't enforce are meaningless. Rules you *can't* uphold cause you to feel out of control and frustrated.

You might tell your teenager, "You will *never* smoke cigarettes."

That's a specific, clear standard, but is it one you can enforce?

No. Not unless you plan to handcuff yourself to your teenager 24/7. How will you enforce that rule when your son or daughter is at school, the mall, or church camp?

A rule you *can* enforce is, "No smoking in my house or in my car. And no cigarette-smelling clothes are allowed in my house, either." You can enforce the rules in your house; it's the right kind of control, back in your hands.

Do I want my teenager to smoke, ever? No. So I teach, mentor, pray, and lead by example, influencing without embarrassment or shame, to that end. But a *rule* about cigarette smoking has to be within my reach of enforcement. And even then, compliance is not guaranteed.

4. *Ask yourself, "Is this a hill worth dying on?"* Is this rule worth all the effort, fight, or confrontation? If it is, fight to win. If it's not worth dying over, keep it as good advice—but don't make it a rule.

Here's a real-life example. A running war was waged in my house for several years when my two daughters, Terryll and Heidi, were teenagers. Well, it was a war for *me*—not for them, nor for my wife.

These mysterious breakfast bowls were being left in various bedrooms, even though the phantom bowl users had to pass through the kitchen on the way to school. I got tired of moving these dirty bowls to the kitchen, but they kept popping up in bedrooms. I could never seem to win the ongoing battle of the bowls.

Since I tend to be a "fix it" person, I made a rule that all breakfast bowls had to be placed in the dishwasher before the girls left the house.

Now, stop right here.

Is it important that dirty dishes be placed in the dishwasher?

Yes.

Does it make logical sense to put your bowl in the dishwasher on your way to the car?

Yes.

Is this a hill worth dying on? Is it worth having to issue a consequence every time the rule is broken?

No.

Is this even an issue of safety or chaos?

Not really.

Yes, it's a good idea to pick up dirty dishes. So I put it in the "advice" category. I frequently reminded my daughters to put their bowls away. But there was no consequence to enforce because there was no rule.

Eventually, something strange happened. The bowls began showing up in the kitchen sink. The sink is exactly 18 inches from the dishwasher; somehow the bowls couldn't make that final leg of the journey.

In an attempt to "control" the situation, I again considered making a rule. But I decided not to.

And guess what? My daughters grew up and got married. The breakfast bowl dilemma is over. They don't live here anymore. Problem solved.

Getting bowls into the dishwasher is good, but not worth making an official rule over. It's worth teaching about and reminding about. But it's not a hill to die on.

Besides, it was a personal issue for me—not about safety or chaos. Unwashed bowls are an annoyance, but they don't qualify as anarchy.

I never got therapy for this, even though my daughters—both holding college degrees in psychology—have hinted that I needed some. I was making a mountain out of a mole hill, and it wasn't even a mole hill worth dying on. "Pick your battles carefully" is a wise saying.

5. *Be sure your motive—your reason for this rule—is a good one.* Keep your goal in mind: to make it "ouch" a bit when your teenager chooses stupid, not to "control" him or make him "turn out right."

If you can downgrade the rule to advice, try doing so. "Violating" advice doesn't require you to mete out consequences, since no law has been broken. Of course, disregarding sound advice might stimulate conversation and teaching.

6. *Realize that some rules will morph into advice as your teenager gets older.* When my daughters were in their early teens, they had to do the following when they wanted to go out: ask and receive permission, then tell us where they were going, who they were going to be with, what they were going to do, and when they were going to be home. They had a curfew, too.

As they moved into their later teenage years, the rule about providing information was "downsized" to the category of advice. We asked them the same questions; if they forgot to leave us a note supplying it, they were reminded to do so next time. But there was no longer a consequence.

Keeping others informed was a wise practice and a courtesy to the rest of the family. My wife, Becky, and I would share this kind of information with our daughters whenever *we* headed out of the house. We were modeling the behavior we wanted them to practice, but also did so because it was respectful.

Not all rules will change as kids get older, of course. But moving an issue from a rule to advice allows you to move from policeman to teacher, mentor, and encourager. That's better than always having to be the "bad guy."

7. *Remember that rules need to be reviewed, updated, and sometimes even dumped.* When Becky and I lived in Arizona in the early '80s, we heard there was a state law saying that no more than three horses could be tied to one hitching post at the same time. I'm not talking about the 1880s; I mean the 1980s!

Are your rules clear and current? Are there any you can expunge from the books to make things simpler and easier for everyone in the family? Could you get rid of "No feeding oatmeal into the VCR" if your kids are 16 and 13 and you haven't touched a videocassette for years? I think so.

Truth and Consequences

Just as a rule needs to be enforceable by you, the consequence for violation needs to be something you can mete out.

One of my counseling clients, a single mom I'll call Martha, had a serious problem with this principle. She banned her two sons, 17-year-old Matthew and 15-year-old Andy, from playing their video games for two weeks. The problem was that the boys got home from school at 2:30 P.M., and Martha didn't make it until after 5:45. How could she enforce the consequence when she wasn't there?

If you can't enforce the consequence, don't give it out.

Still, Martha was one tenacious lady. She outsmarted her boys by putting a small padlock through a hole in the TV plug. With the padlock in place, her sons couldn't put the plug in the socket.

Score one for Mom. But her sons were smart, too. They cut off the factory-molded plug and wired on a different one from the hardware store.

This teen victory would have gone undetected, but Martha came home early one day and found Matt and Andy engrossed in their favorite video game. She locked the entire video system in her bedroom closet.

After a couple of days, Matt and Andy discovered where the system was hidden, managed to pick the lock, played games for a few hours, and returned the system to the "locked" closet before Mom got home. They even performed a whining act, begging their mother to *pleeeeze* let them have their game system back.

Eventually Martha figured out what was going on. At this point I reminded her, "Do what you can, not what you can't." I asked her if this was a hill worth dying on.

It wasn't, because she couldn't enforce the consequence when she was physically absent. Make no mistake: She wanted to be a good mom, to honor God in the way she raised her sons. She was doing a good job of single parenting, not looking for an easy way out.

If this had been a hill Martha was willing to die on, she could have carried the game system to work and left it there. But that hinged on the assumption that she could physically get out of the house with the system in hand.

Matt and Andy were taller and stronger than Martha, and we guessed they would take it to the point of a physical altercation if she tried to remove the console. We considered calling police to escort Martha out the door with the video system—but decided (wisely, I believe) to drop the battle, regroup, and live to fight another day.

Another key principle is to make sure consequences are specific and limited. Some parents dish out a consequence with no clean end to it, attaching a phrase like, "You have to earn it back." If you choose to ground your son, make sure there's a clear time limit. If you take the cell phone away from your daughter, make sure she knows which day she'll get it back.

The reason is simple. Consequences make it "ouch" a bit after a stupid choice. Adding a vague "When you're responsible enough, then we'll . . ." or "When we see your behavior change, then . . ." usually means you're trying to control behavior rather than making an "ouch" point.

A final principle is to keep the consequence connected to the broken rule.

Dale's 16-year-old son, Tommy, wasn't motivated about school or grades. But Dale and his wife, Beth, had a long-standing rule: "Earn at least a 3.0 grade point average every semester." Their system of awarding Tommy money for every A and B suddenly stopped working when Tommy got a part-time job and started making his own money. What to do?

As I talked with Dale, I learned that Tommy was very motivated about getting to drive the family car. Dale's insurance company offered a good-driver discount for teens who had a 3.0 grade point average or above. Dale was paying Tommy's insurance as an "add-on" to the existing family policy.

After getting the numbers, Dale told Tommy the following.

Rule: Get at least a 3.0 grade point average every semester in school.

Consequence: If you don't maintain the grades required for the insurance company's discount, you'll have to pay the difference between the good-driver rate and the higher rate. If you don't pay the difference, you can either buy your own policy or lose your driver's license—since in Colorado, all licensed drivers must carry insurance.

Driving the family car was directly tied to Tommy's grades by the law of cause and effect.

Right about now you may be saying, "Wait. I thought you said rules were to keep safety in and chaos out. What's a kid's GPA got to do with safety?"

Nothing.

I didn't say Dale's 3.0 rule was good. In fact, at the time I disagreed with it—as a *rule.* I do think it's a great piece of *advice,* and that a parent might use the insurance-rate deal, not as a consequence, but as a learning experience.

But as I've also stated, "It's your house. It's your rules."

Just be smart with your rules. And learn to separate rules, advice, and suggestions.

Giving Grace—or Is It Mercy?

With all this talk about rules and consequences, where does grace fit in? If you're a Christian, aren't you supposed to extend grace toward others?

In addressing that question, let me offer simple definitions of grace and mercy.

Grace is *getting* something I *do not* deserve.

Mercy is *not* getting something I *do* deserve.

When your teenager deserves consequences for breaking a rule—but doesn't get them—we're talking about mercy rather than grace.

Mercy and consequences—and rules, for that matter—aren't incompatible. If rules are to keep safety in and chaos out, then making rules qualifies as an act of love as well as an act of grace.

If your primary reason for doling out a consequence is to make it "ouch" a little when your teenager makes an unsafe choice, you're attempting to *influence* his or her future choices. Good for you. Isn't that also an act of love and grace?

So where does *mercy* come into play? Is there a good time to dispense mercy to your teenager instead of the predetermined consequence? Here's a suggestion from one parent to another.

I extend mercy when I see in my daughter's eyes that she "gets it," that she really internalizes the lesson learned from her poor choice. I extend mercy when I see that applying the consequence—which she seems willing to accept—won't help her "get it" any more than she's already "gotten it."

Under those circumstances I'm more than willing to *not* give her the consequence she deserves. I extend mercy because the lesson that needs to be learned is being learned. Mission accomplished.

What about cases when you don't want to deal with an issue, so you cop out by telling your teenager you'll extend grace "this time"? That's not extending grace. It's not even extending mercy, because you're acting out of your own interest rather than in the interest of your teenager.

Be sure your motive is healthy as you consider granting mercy. Carefully extending mercy can provide a powerful illustration of God's mercy given to all of us. Avoiding an unpleasant confrontation and labeling it "mercy" is a lie. And only the truth will set us free.

Rules and Respect

Some house rules are designed to discourage being disrespectful toward you or other family members. It's important to address the issue of respect in your house rules because it's about safety—emotional and mental safety. Disrespect can cause chaos, too.

But it's also important to define disrespect carefully. The most common definition seems to be, "anything you're doing that I don't want you to be doing right now." Here are some examples:

- Mark says his 15-year-old son, Jeremy, is being disrespectful because he's disagreeing with Mark's 10:30 P.M. curfew and is talking back. Jeremy says he's just trying to discuss the issue like an adult, and that he has a right to differ with his father.
- Donna points her finger and cries, "Disrespect!" whenever her 13-year-old daughter rolls her eyes and says, "Whatever, Mom."
- Lane, a father of four children between the ages of 13 and 19, feels strongly that any show of anger is disrespectful—no matter how family members choose to express that anger.
- When single-mom Jessica asks her teenage son to do a chore, he often replies, "I'll do it later." She feels disrespected because her request isn't met with immediate obedience.

Are these really cases of disrespect? Are rules needed to remedy the situation?

Here's an exercise to help you decide how to deal with disrespect in your home. Take out a piece of paper and write clear definitions of respect and disrespect. Here's a starter list to help you with the latter. Disrespect is:

- physical violence, or threats of same
- physical posturing, bullying
- destruction of property, or threats thereof
- cursing at someone

- name-calling
- condemnations ("I hate you!")

Take out a dictionary and compare its definitions with yours. You'll probably find that disrespect is both an action and an attitude.

Rules address disrespectful *actions*, keeping safety in and chaos out. Advice, teaching, and mentoring address disrespectful *attitudes*. You need both. Just be sure to keep them separate.

Working with other family members, clarify your household definition of disrespect. Then, if you want rules, write them. Be sure they focus on specific actions; attitudes will be addressed with teaching and mentoring.

And modeling, too. House rules are for everyone to follow, especially when it comes to showing respect for each other. Mom and Dad are to follow the rules as well. It's hard to enforce regulations that you refuse to obey yourself.

Lead by example first. Enforce rules second.

Take Five

Here's one more exercise that could change the way your family uses rules.

If you could have only *five* household rules, what would they be?

Make a written list. Be sure your rules are specific, clear, and enforceable. Cover everything you deem important for safety. But you can have only five.

And no rule is allowed to have 65 sub-rules!

I gave this assignment to Gary and Rita when I was helping them work with their 16-year-old son. Rita came back a week later with nine typewritten pages. There were only five numbered rules, per my instructions, but each rule had multiple sub-rules.

Rita was trying to pack as much into those five regulations as she could. Her real motive was to control her son Jared's every behavior and attitude.

I sent Rita and Gary home to try again, asking them to create five simple, clear rules. By the next appointment, Rita had pared her nine pages down to three. "It was the best I could do," she said.

Still, she had too many sneaky addendums to each rule. After talking about the reason for rules and Rita's reasons for her three pages, I sent the couple home yet again with the same assignment.

By the end of the third session, Rita and Gary finally understood. They wrestled with their motives for controlling Jared. They came to see that they couldn't control him, that it wasn't their job, and that they could make and enforce rules to keep safety in and chaos out.

What will your five rules be? Separate them from principles you choose to teach. Also, make a list of important items that fall into the "suggestions" category.

There's nothing magical or "psychological" about the number five. The purpose is to help you think small—as well as simply, clearly, and specifically. You may end up with a few more than five rules, and that's fine. Just let me emphasize the word "few." Make sure these rules are clear in your own mind so that you can state them plainly to your children.

In writing rules, focus on the things you *can* control and influence rather than the things you *can't* control. Effective rules use the HOLD style of interacting—encouraging family members to take responsibility for things they can control. Rules that GRAB—trying to take responsibility for things you can't control—are doomed to fail.

Need help getting started on your list? Here's a sample rule from the Sanford household:

"Follow the civil laws (national, state, and municipal)." This means you'll need to know what those laws are, so you know what to enforce and when a law has been broken. Be sure to do your homework first. This "specific" rule may sound like it has 732 addendums—which I suggested you *not* do. But in this case, it makes sense. Besides, there's an exception to every rule, right?

And remember—household rules like this are for everyone in the family to follow.

NINE

When They Make You So Mad (and Vice Versa)

Mention the words *control* and *teenager* in the same sentence, and it usually isn't long before the issue of anger crops up.

Anger is the emotion many of us parents—especially those who are Christians—have the hardest time dealing with in healthy ways. Are you afraid to admit that you get angry frequently? Are you afraid to see your teenager get angry? Some people, often those from a Christian background, are raised in an atmosphere where anger is suppressed. They never learn how to deal with it directly.

Anger represents a broad continuum of emotion ranging from a feeling of annoyance to pure, out-of-control rage. States like "frustration" and "being upset" fall somewhere in between. The milder forms of anger may be acceptable and less threatening, but the wilder forms are often too scary for us to deal with effectively, so we try to shut them down.

"But what's anger got to do with helping me 'lose control' of my teenager and like it?" you might ask.

When anger becomes action, it often focuses on trying to force an outcome or control a circumstance or person. Often that target is a teenager or his or her behaviors.

Here are a few reasons why *anger*, *control*, and *teenager* belong in the same sentence—and in this chapter:

- When you're afraid to feel or express anger as a parent, you're tempted to GRAB control of your teen to keep misbehavior from "making you mad."
- When you're afraid of your teen's anger, you're tempted to GRAB control in order to keep him from expressing it.
- When you dispense a consequence and your teen gets angry, you're tempted to GRAB responsibility and back down.
- When your teen's behavior leaves you angry, you're tempted to lose faith in influence and revert to control.

You can avoid these pitfalls by learning healthy ways to handle anger—yours and your teen's. That begins with understanding the real sources of anger.

Where Anger Comes From

Anger is neither bad nor good, and can be misused and misinterpreted easily. It can also have a very destructive side. Maybe that's why we tend to fear it.

It's a secondary emotion; it comes into being by combining two other emotions. Here's the simple formula: *Hurt + Worry = Anger*.

Whenever you mix vinegar and baking soda, you get bubbles. Whenever you mix hurt (disappointment, pain, loss) and worry (the "what if" thinking covered in Chapter 6), you get anger (frustration, rage, annoyance).

The formula works the same for parents as it does for teenagers. If you're angry, you usually have hurt and worry going on inside. Let's look at each component separately.

The Hurt Feelings

Hurt is sadness, letdown, pain—the "bummer" part of life. This isn't some deep psychological issue stemming from "how you were potty trained"; it's reacting to an event that bothers you physically, emotionally, or relationally. It may remind you of similar feelings from the past, but there's always a present tense to any hurt you're feeling.

What part of life hasn't gone the way you expected or wanted? What hope or dream has been or is being shattered? Questions like these can help you—and your teen—understand the "hurt" ingredient of anger.

I can't give you a formula that takes away hurt. We live in a broken, fallen world and will all experience pain. But as parents we can teach and model for our teenagers how to deal with pain and sadness.

For some people, it helps to cry and talk about hurts. One mom I know finds that approach works for her—but not necessarily for her teenage son. Here's what happened when her son, Rich, didn't make the varsity tennis team:

> I was out of town on business, but heard that Rich felt pretty bad about things and was in his room with the door shut. He played his guitar and mostly stayed away from everybody else that night. He and his dad did have a talk, and Rich said a little about his disappointment.
>
> Rich had tried so hard to make the team, taking private lessons and practicing all summer. I felt terrible about it. Finally I talked with him when I got home. "I'm really sorry you didn't get on varsity like you wanted to," I told him.
>
> "I know," he said.
>
> I was surprised he didn't say more. "I just feel bad for you," I continued. "You know, I empathize."
>
> "What's that mean?" he asked, sounding doubtful.

"It means I'm trying to feel your pain," I said in my most motherly, nurturing way.

His reply came in that "Mom, you're embarrassing me" tone parents of teens hear so often. "Well, I wish you wouldn't," he replied.

Somehow he managed to move on with his life. It took me a little longer.

Every parent and every teen reacts to hurt in his or her own way, of course. For some, the disappointment runs so deep that counseling is needed.

Many of us parents, "feeling the pain" of our teens, want to make it stop—for ourselves and for them. We try to "fix" the situation by GRABing control. But the two healthy styles of interacting are HOLD and FOLD.

The Worry Feelings

If you feel angry, there's a "what if" lurking in your thinking—whether or not you're aware of it.

Imagine you have a three-year-old named Micah. You tell him it's time for his afternoon nap, and he blows up in a tantrum. What's his "hurt"? He has to stop playing.

But what's his worry?

Think like a three-year-old here. Taking a one-hour nap in the middle of the day seems like sleeping away half your lifetime. Without being fully aware of it, he wonders:

- *What if something really cool happens and I don't get to be part of it?*
- *What if my toys disappear while I'm asleep?*
- *What if Mommy leaves me?*

When the hurt mixes with the worry, Micah is angry.

The same formula fits if you're a six-foot-three football player for the

Denver Broncos and you get pulled from your middle linebacker position after a missed tackle. You feel angry.

What's the hurt? Instead of playing the game, you have to sit on the bench and watch someone else in your position.

What's the worry?

- *What if Coach doesn't put me back in the game?*
- *What if my sub outplays me and I lose my starting position?*
- *What if I lose my chance for commercial endorsements because of this?*

Worry lures too many of us parents into the GRAB style of interacting. In an attempt to quiet our anxiety and avoid the catastrophe that our "what if" thinking has conjured up, we're tempted to step in and GRAB ownership of what's not ours to control. To learn how to deal with this ingredient of anger, see Chapter 6.

The Angry Feelings

When dealing with your teenager, you might find that your anger flares up and is difficult to control. You may think the solution is controlling your teen and the entire situation, but it's not. Don't move into GRABing. HOLD on to your own feelings of anger first, taking responsibility for them.

What then? There are two rules for what *not* to do when you're angry, and they apply to parents *and* teenagers:

1. *Don't hurt others.* Don't hit, attack, or threaten to hurt another person. Don't hurt with words by yelling or name-calling. Don't damage someone else's stuff (turning china plates into Frisbees, for instance).

2. *Don't hurt yourself.* Don't cut yourself, slam your fist into the wall, or even overexercise with weights. Don't call yourself names or beat yourself up verbally. Don't damage your own stuff by tearing up your favorite pictures or throwing your iPod across the room.

In other words, don't let anger make you disrespectful toward anyone—others or yourself.

Being angry isn't wrong. Expressing anger isn't wrong. It's *how* anger is expressed that can be right or wrong, smart or stupid. Choose smart ways to express and deal with your anger in order to avoid the "ouch" that will come if you choose stupid.

Some people think it's impossible to express anger without breaking those two rules. One father and adult son, both with anger issues, told me after hearing what to avoid, "There's nothing left to do!"

Not true. You just need to get a little creative. Here are a few ideas that have worked for my clients over the years:

- Ben buried his face in the pillow on his bed and screamed. It didn't hurt anybody else's ears, and didn't hurt him.
- Glen, 17, closed the door to his room and played his acoustic guitar.
- Zoë, an adult, got into her car, drove up the interstate, and screamed at the top of her lungs. Passing drivers thought she was just singing along with the radio. When she got the anger out she turned around, played some mellow music, and had a calm drive home. (Note: Don't use driving itself as an expression of anger, which endangers yourself and others.)
- Several found it helpful to write in journals.
- Some did something physical—lifted weights, went for a walk or run, or cleaned the house, garage, or kitchen.
- Others called a friend and "talked things out."
- Counting to 10 worked for some.
- Some squeezed a "stress ball." I have a "forearm trainer donut" from a mountaineering store that would work perfectly.

The important thing is to work out a plan, choosing your response in advance—before you actually get angry.

That was the case with 15-year-old Paul, with whom I worked on anger management. He decided to walk around the block the next time he got angry, knowing that it would never work for him to say, "Mother, I'm extremely angry right now; can we have a pleasant conversation about this emotion I'm experiencing?" He needed to do something physical.

His plan worked, though one night things got a little out of hand. He grew angry around 10:45, left the house, and didn't return until 2:00 in the morning. He'd been walking around the block the whole time, but he'd also broken his midnight curfew. His mom and I complimented him on defusing his anger in a healthy way and controlling himself—though he did get a consequence for breaking the rule. His mom extended mercy by cutting the consequence in half, and he accepted both the validation and the penalty.

Don't Let Anger Take Control

If it's your teenager who needs help dealing with anger, what will be most effective for him or her?

Rather than giving an answer, ask your son or daughter that question. Let him or her wrestle with it and take some ownership of the situation.

The same is true of you. Instead of wishing your teen would just stop "making you mad," ask yourself what would help you express and handle anger in healthy ways. If you can't answer that, don't hesitate to get advice from a pastor or counselor.

Anger is not an emotion to shy away from. It's also not one that deserves to shape your relationship with your teenager. Dealing with the hurts and worries that produce anger, and expressing it appropriately, is a much better strategy than letting it incite a battle for control.

TEN

Intervention: When You Have to Step In

- Jean is deeply worried about her 14-year-old daughter, Missy. In the past six months Missy has lost 25 pounds. At first she looked great without her usual baby fat, but now she seems too thin and acts obsessed with her weight and exercise program. Jean wonders if Missy has crossed the line from health-conscious to anorexic or bulimic. When Jean mentions Missy's lack of interest in food, the girl withdraws and refuses to talk. What can Jean do?

- Bill suspects his son, Alan, has started going to drinking parties. The 16-year-old comes home with alcohol on his breath and collapses into bed. It's nearly impossible to get Alan up for school, and on weekends he sleeps half the day. Bill has confronted the teen a few times, but got only angry denials in return. Bill knows he has to do something before his son becomes a confirmed alcoholic.

- Betsy is out of ideas when it comes to her son, Sam, who's lived with her since her divorce five years ago. The 17-year-old has dropped out of school and can't seem to hold a simple job. He comes home late at night reeking of marijuana. She's forbidden him to use drugs or bring them home, but knows he's ignoring her. Afraid he'll end up in jail, she doesn't want to throw him out of the house. She cries herself to sleep each night wondering where to go for help.

- Sixteen-year-old Wendy didn't come home last night. Her parents, frantic with worry, were ready to phone police when they received a call from their daughter: "I'm staying with Craig. We love each other and you can't keep us apart anymore." Craig, 17, lives with an older brother, holds a low-paying job, and still has a few classes to finish before he can graduate. Wendy's parents wonder how to keep their daughter from getting pregnant or dropping out of school.

Drugs, alcohol, sex, eating disorders—so many traps can capture a teenager before a parent fully realizes there's a serious problem. What happens when your teenager *is* totally out of control? Do ideas like HOLD, FOLD, and influence still apply?

This Is a Job for . . .

When to step in and intervene—and how—is not always clear. There aren't always straightforward answers to a parent's frantic questions. I'll start, though, with two responses to the query about what to do when your teenager is out of control.

First, seek help sooner rather than later. Parents often wait too long, hoping the situation will fix itself. Sometimes things *are* resolved on their own, but sometimes they only get worse. This chapter offers a look at your options, so you'll know where to go for help. You don't have to reach for a therapist at the first sign of trouble, but you do need to reach out. If the level of help you enlist successfully addresses the situation, great. If it doesn't do the job, seek the next level.

Second, find assistance when your teenager's behavior is . . .

- intense *enough* and on the verge of dangerous, or
- marked by *enough* major behavioral and/or personality changes that can't be otherwise defined, or
- disruptive *enough* to everyday routine that he or she isn't operating as he or she normally can.

I emphasize *enough* in each of these three statements, realizing it's a very subjective term. If you're concerned, yet uncertain about your ability to resolve the problem, it's time to get help.

Where do you look? This chapter provides an overview of mental health and other services available to aid teenagers. Some would call it a "continuum of care."

That's the term for a wide range of services for problems that vary from mild to severe. The idea is to begin with the least restrictive form of service—that is, the form that restricts a teen's freedom least—and move to others only as needed.

Here you'll find a general overview of the continuum of care available in the United States; comparable programs may be offered in some other countries. Names of agencies may vary from state to state, but general services will be similar. The list may seem more detailed than you need at the moment, but we'll cover the entire continuum in case one option meets your individual need. The list begins with services that are least restrictive and moves to those that are most restrictive.

"But what does all this have to do with losing control of my teenager?" you might ask. "Isn't intervention an attempt to control?"

No. By seeking help, you're admitting you can't "fix" this yourself. You're not trying to GRAB control; you're FOLDing your hands. With outside assistance, you're attempting to influence your son or daughter more effectively.

You're not giving up on your teenager. You're not a failure as a parent. You're "regrouping" and upping the intensity of your influence. The outcome is still in the hands of God and your teenager.

You can't fight Rule One and win. That's a load off your back. But you can activate Rule Three by making things "ouch" a little—or a lot—because of your teen's choices.

Parental Involvement

Your first line of defense is *you*. Stay involved in your teenager's business in good ways and for appropriate reasons. That's what you're doing by reading this book, and why you try to maintain regular, personal contact with your teen.

Remember, teenagers take as much of their parents' time as they did when they were toddlers (though in different ways). Now you need to be involved through avenues that are acceptable to your teenager so you're not always annoying him or her. Sometimes teens need to be annoyed, but only when necessary. The rest of the time, try to keep your involvement "acceptable," based on your son's or daughter's personality.

Mentoring and Youth Groups

This help could come from a youth pastor or youth worker at your church, a leader from a group like Young Life or Athletes in Action, a sports coach, or a similar influencer. More formal mentoring situations include life coaching, a support group offered by a school counselor, or an assigned sponsor at a local Alcoholics Anonymous meeting.

The goal is to have a healthy adult engage with your teenager and share words of wisdom and common sense with him or her. More formal mentoring, especially life coaching, usually requires a fee for services.

Mentors may say *exactly the same things* you've been saying as a parent. But since they aren't "the parent," their words may actually be heard by your teen. I know that's not fair, but it's often the way it is. Relax; at least your teen is hearing the right things (again) from a reliable source.

Remember Bill and Betsy, whose teens Alan and Sam were getting involved with alcohol and marijuana? Mentoring could be a good first step for them. Finding healthy adults to speak into your teenager's life is often the place to start. But for many parents, it's not the place to stop.

Outpatient Therapy

This is what most people think of when they consider "counseling." It involves one to three hours per week spent with a licensed therapist or psychologist. This may consist of individual therapy (the teenager meets with the therapist), family therapy (the therapist meets with the entire family), or group therapy (clients of similar ages with a common diagnosis or issue, as in an anger management group, meet with a therapist).

Here are a few points to consider when thinking about this option.

Therapists can be found in a variety of locations, including churches. Some churches have licensed professional counselors on staff; some provide referrals for Christian therapists in the community. If you need help finding a counselor in your area, Focus on the Family has a referral network of Christian therapists. For information, call (719) 531-3400 and ask for the counseling department.

Some agencies offer services for people needing financial assistance. A county mental health center, for example, might provide therapy on a sliding scale. This would be secular counseling, unless there's a therapist on staff who handles issues of faith. Some church denominations have community centers providing counseling services at low fees or no fees. Often these have phrases like "community services" or "family services" in their names.

A private therapist starting a new practice may offer reduced fees in order to establish a client base. More established therapists may still offer a sliding scale if needed.

It's wise to conduct a telephone interview with a therapist before making an initial appointment. Some therapists are more comfortable with a face-to-face interview, and that's fine, too. In addition to getting specifics about professional credentials, fees, insurance information, and days and times available for appointments, be sure to ask the following:

- What's your specific counseling theory? (If necessary, ask the therapist to explain what it means in terms you can understand.)
- Do you just do "reflective listening," or do you engage the client with questions and challenge his or her thinking when appropriate?
- Do you do an assessment and diagnosis workup?
- Do you have specific therapeutic goals that you and the client agree to?
- Do you develop a treatment plan (written or not) to help the client reach those goals?

When working with a teenager, you'll benefit if you have a therapist who takes the following steps.

1. *Here's where you are.* The therapist does a good assessment and diagnostic workup.

2. *Here's where we're going.* The therapist develops specific treatment goals that the teen and parents agree on.

3. *Here's how we'll get there.* The therapist develops a treatment plan. It may be formalized or fluid, but it's important that it be specific and that everyone involved (therapist, teenager, and parents) is aware of it. This keeps the therapy on task and allows evaluation of whether progress is being made.

Though these steps may seem obvious, don't assume all therapists think or operate this way. Psychology is a very broad field with many different therapeutic styles and forms.

In fact, *any* question is fair game when interviewing a potential therapist. If the counselor finds the question too personal, he or she can simply respond, "I don't give out that information about myself." I've been asked many questions over the years; here are a few.

- "How old are you?"
- "Are you married? For how many years?"

- "Have you been divorced?"
- "Do you have teenagers of your own?"
- "What church (or denomination) do you attend?"
- "What sort of involvement do you have at your church?"
- "How will you keep me involved in the counseling process?"
- "How will I know when I'm 'done' with therapy?"

Your aim in this interview is to get as good a "fit" as possible with the therapist. Though it isn't a guarantee, it can save time and money down the road. If a therapist is not willing to provide a no-charge interview before making the first appointment, go somewhere else. Therapy is a business, after all. You're the customer.

Once you begin working with a therapist, you're not "stuck" seeing him or her forever. If things aren't working out, or the situation has changed and this therapist doesn't have the expertise to continue, move on. Pay your bill, say "Thank you," and look for another therapist. It's business, not personal.

Realize, though, that the best therapist in the world can't "fix" your teenager. The wild card of free will is a fact of life for counselors as well as parents.

Sometimes a therapist needs to involve other professionals. Because of Jean's concern over Missy's possible eating disorder, for example, I encouraged Jean to get in touch right away with a specialist trained to evaluate and work with anorexia and bulimia. In the cases of substance abusers Alan and Sam, their parents may need a chemical dependency evaluation done by a specialist. Depending on how the evaluation turns out, the therapist may work with the teens or refer them to an intensive outpatient program—the next step in our continuum of care.

Intensive Outpatient Program

An IOP usually is operated by a local hospital. A teenager attends three to five days per week, usually in the afternoon or evening, for two to three hours per day. Therapy often includes a mix of group therapy, psycho-educational groups (teaching sessions), individual therapy, and sometimes family therapy. The program is often quite structured, yet allows flexibility to "wrap" services around each person as necessary. Most IOPs center on either chemical dependency (CD) or sex offenses (JSOP, or juvenile sex-offender program).

If your teenager has been ordered by a court into therapy for a specific offense, you may be looking at some kind of IOP. There usually will be a fee for services.

Sometimes teens enter IOPs as a result of other counseling. For instance, Pamela brought her 14-year-old son, Gary, to see me for an evaluation. He had been inappropriately touching his 5-year-old sister for some time.

For Pamela, step one was my office—outpatient therapy for Gary, her daughter, and herself. State law required me to report Gary's behavior, and I shared with Gary and Pamela what they might expect next.

Gary went to court and was ordered into a JSOP. Knowing two Christian therapists on the state-sanctioned list, I referred Pamela to them. She and Gary were relieved that the JSOP facilitators had a similar belief system. Since I don't work with younger children, I referred Pamela to an outpatient therapist who would counsel her daughter—and was able to assist Pamela with her own grief, anger, and worry.

Day Treatment Program

A day treatment program is an educational setting—often operated by a school district—in which a teenager attends class five days a week and receives academic credit. Therapy, usually group and individual, is included in the daily routine. Other services are available if something happens during the day that warrants intervention. Day treatment programs that are part of the public school system usually don't have out-of-pocket fees attached to them.

Since this kind of program is centered on the education of your teenager, he or she probably will be placed here after a recommendation from school staff. Rather than being the first option for your teenager, this will likely come after other services have failed.

Living with a Relative or Friend

This is usually the first step toward moving a teenager out of the home. Up to this point, the other services operate with your teenager still residing with you. With this option, if you're free of legal mandates, you arrange for your teenager to live with a family member or friend.

There are several reasons why you might decide to do this. Perhaps you have younger children who are endangered by your teen's out-of-control behavior, but Uncle John with a ranch in Montana doesn't. Sometimes—and for no clear reason—a teenager will do better just because he or she is no longer under the direct authority of his or her parents.

If you're considering this, be sure to prepare written permissions so that the relative or friend can get medical care for your teen. You'll also want to discuss financial reimbursement. You may also want to arrange formal outpatient therapy for your teen while he or she lives with the relative or friend.

Be sure you're not taking your teen out of the frying pan only to place him or her in the fire. Is the relative or friend healthy enough physically and emotionally to handle your teenager's present condition?

Living with a friend or relative might be the next step for Sam, the 17-year-old mentioned at the beginning of this chapter. Depending on how he behaves toward Betsy, she may not be able to handle him effectively. If there are friends or relatives who would be able and willing to take Sam, they might provide the support, structure, and boundaries he needs.

This kind of arrangement is the first thing I'd recommend for the parents of Wendy, the 16-year-old who'd decided to move in with her boyfriend. The reason? To get her as far away as possible from her environment—and the boy.

Living with Your Ex-spouse

While this is not an official service, it's an option to weigh if it applies. Again, it's an out-of-home placement, by your design.

Many parents I've known had to choose the "lesser of two evils" when thinking about having a teenager live with his or her other parent. But there are times when this arrangement needs to be considered.

If you do place your son or daughter with the other parent, it's best to formalize this change in parental responsibilities with the court. Seek legal counsel before proceeding.

For Betsy, this was the option she finally had to settle on. She sent Sam to live with his father, who owned a ranch in the Northwest. This was not an easy choice for her, but it was the smart one.

Foster Home

A foster placement puts a teenager into the "system"—either the legal system or Child Welfare Services (often known as Child Protective Services). Foster homes are long-term placements with foster parents in charge, much like a traditional home setting. The number of foster children is kept to a minimum, governed by state guidelines. In "therapeutic" foster homes, foster parents have specific training in mental health issues; additional services such as medications and therapy may be available.

Some foster home programs accept private placements. In such cases, you could take the initiative to work with the organization and formally place your teenager. The catch: Unless a court order mandates that your teenager goes into placement, he or she will need to voluntarily sign into that program. Usually the age for voluntary sign-in for a minor is around 15, though it may vary from state to state. For this reason, most foster home placements are part of the judicial or Child Protective Services system.

A foster child attends either a public or private school—or, in some cases, may be home schooled by the foster parents.

If your teenager is officially in the social services or juvenile justice system, often fees for placement are covered by county or state funds. This is true for foster homes, group homes, and residential facilities, which we'll cover next. A private placement to any of these programs probably will require you to foot the bill.

Group Home

Group homes also offer long-term placement and have a larger number of residents—usually five to eight, depending on state guidelines. Parents in these homes generally are given periodic respites by other caregivers.

These homes provide therapy, usually group and individual. Some require monthly family therapy as well.

A slightly different arrangement is found in specialized group centers. These facilities are staffed around the clock, seven days a week. Their therapeutic services are more intense—group therapy (possibly with several specialized groups), individual therapy, and family therapy sessions.

The resident count for a specialized group center, which may be as large as 12, is regulated by state guidelines to ensure a good staff-to-resident ratio.

With either type of group home, educational services are provided. Often a teen attends a local public school that offers programs designed to meet his or her special needs.

Residential Child Care Facility

A residential child care facility (RCCF) accepts long-term placement; it provides 24-hour supervision and even more services than facilities mentioned so far. This includes group therapy, specialized group therapy, individual therapy, and family therapy.

Teenagers in an RCCF may attend a community-based Alcoholics Anonymous meeting once a week, if appropriate. RCCFs are required to have an educational component, so that residents can keep working toward their high school diplomas or GEDs.

Wendy, the 16-year-old who'd moved in with her boyfriend, came to reside in an RCCF. There were no friends or relatives with whom she could live. (This is not unusual; it's rare for the friends-and-relatives option to work out, though I still encourage parents to check into it.) Wendy's parents chose a Christian facility in another state, using the influencing power of geographic distance to their advantage.

Residential Treatment Center

A residential treatment center (RTC) is a staff-secured program; each resident is to be in sight of a staff member 24 hours a day. It features a high staff-to-resident ratio and more in-depth therapeutic services than an RCCF provides. As a result, it can handle a broader spectrum of more severe diagnoses.

RTCs often include "wrap around" services, such as a transition home for residents leaving the RTC and reintegrating into society, emancipation programs for those who'll be on their own upon leaving the facility, and job training.

Teens with major rebellion and behavioral issues often need RTC placement. So do those with a "dual diagnosis"—a behavioral or psychological condition and a chemical dependency (CD). RTCs also can deal with more difficult cases of post-traumatic stress disorder (PTSD), abandonment issues, developmental delays, ADHD, abuse, *plus* CD issues.

If your teenager is in the legal system, it may be possible for you to recommend to the court that he or she be placed in an RTC program you've selected. You'll need to find out which programs are compatible with your beliefs and are approved to take state (and out-of-state) placements. I mention this because RTC programs can be very expensive; if your son or daughter receives a court-ordered placement, there may be county or state funds available to help.

If your teenager is over the age of 15 (this varies from state to state), he may need to sign himself in to enter an RTC program. Those who are court-ordered have no option to sign or not sign. Sometimes they must choose between RTC or the Department of Youth Corrections.

Youth Detention Center

This is a short-term holding facility, often known as juvenile detention or "juvie." The legal system—not a parent—places a teenager here.

Department of Youth Corrections

DYC, as it is often called, is the legal department that oversees incarceration—long-term commitments for minors. Again, the judicial system is the governing power that places your teenager here.

Medical Hospitalization, Acute

This involves psychiatric hospitalization with a short stay of one to five days. Fees for services are paid by the parent, health insurance provider, or both.

The main goal of an acute, inpatient stay is to stabilize the patient, get her started on medications that may be needed, and develop a discharge plan to get her connected with services that can address the underlying issues. Don't expect those issues to be taken care of in this sort of environment; there's not enough time.

This is where you'll go if your teenager is suicidal or has just attempted suicide. The hospital also can evaluate whether a person is depressed enough or "out of touch with reality" enough that further hospitalization is warranted.

State Hospital

This provides long-term treatment for severe mental health and/or behavioral issues. Most state hospital placements are done by the county or state—the "system." Funding most likely would be covered by the jurisdiction making the placement.

It's not common to be placed in a state hospital. This is the "last resort" when all other forms of care have failed and there is no other program for this person.

Emancipation and Relinquishing Parental Rights

While this option is not exactly a "service of care," it's the final step some parents have had to choose when dealing with a seriously out-of-control teenager. In all my years of working with teenagers, I've walked this path with parents only twice.

This is a legal step, subject to state laws. Legal counsel is necessary when considering it.

This severe intervention is sometimes necessary when all other possibilities have failed. Remember the discussion in Chapter 5 about responsibility versus liability? As long as your teenager is a minor and under your guardianship, you're liable for his or her actions. Relinquishing parental rights or emancipation eliminates your liability and places it on your teenager. Sometimes this is reason enough to consider such a last-ditch effort.

Continuum Confusion

When you have an especially difficult teenager, the journey toward getting help is anything but nice, clean, and neat. If this is your situation, you may be wondering, "What do I do now?"

That question must have run frequently through the mind of Melissa's mother. Melissa (or Mel, as she demanded to be called) was admitted to a residential treatment center, where I was assigned to be her case manager. Mel had already been in individual and family outpatient therapy for some time, but nothing was helping. She was just as defiant as before, if not more so. Finally she'd attempted suicide, which landed her in the adolescent acute unit of a psychiatric hospital. From there she was moved to my facility.

Discharged several months later, Mel returned to individual and family outpatient therapy. Still, there was no curbing her out-of-control behavior. She ran away from home repeatedly; after another suicide attempt, she ended up back on the adolescent acute unit of the psychiatric hospital for the third time. Discharged again, she was placed in a day treatment program. She was attending outpatient therapy when she decided to quit.

During the two and a half years just described, four different types of services were tried: outpatient therapy (individual and family), acute psychiatric hospitalization (three times), a residential treatment center, and a day treatment program. If Mel's mom felt worn out, it was no wonder.

I met up again with Mel's mother. She asked what she should do next. Mel was now 17, still living at home, running the show with out-of-control behavior, terrorizing her older sister and her single mom equally.

Mel would not cooperate with anyone. She refused to live with any other family member; understandably, she refused to have anything to do with the stepfather who'd abused her in the past. She would not voluntarily sign herself into any group or residential program (which would have been necessary, since no court decisions required her to enter). She would not accept any suggestions or rules her mother made. Mel's behavior was destroying the household; it was clearly an issue of safety, both physically and mentally.

Mel was pressing her mother to emancipate her, but Colorado didn't have an official emancipation law. The alternative we chose was for her mother to relinquish parental rights where Mel was concerned. This meant Mom had to take a "hit" by having a dependency and neglect charge filed against her, which went on her record. The state of Colorado then took over guardianship of Mel.

The state could have court-ordered Mel into a group or foster home. But because of her age (over 17 and a half by now), it let her go as an independent citizen—in effect emancipating her.

It was the best decision in a very difficult and painful case—the lesser of two evils. Mel's mom needed lots of support and encouragement; it's not an easy decision for any parent to make.

I lost contact with Mel. Last I heard, her mother did, too. I don't know the end of that story.

But I've known lots of parents like Mel's mother. You, too, may be one who longs to know how your son's or daughter's story will turn out.

Where to Turn

The continuum of care starts with people you already know: a youth pastor, friends, teachers, school counselors, and so on. You can find these people fairly easily. If you need more intervention, it's likely these people will know whom to turn to next.

Youth leaders or pastors will probably know a few good Christian therapists in town. School teachers and counselors usually know therapists who work well with teen issues. Outpatient therapists will know residential services in the region. The continuum is also your "Rolodex" of whom to seek out for the next contact information.

Trying to find the one "right" program that will "fix" your teenager, though, will only frustrate you. Remember, your teen has the right to choose stupid—and to *keep* choosing stupid his entire life if he wants to. Even the best therapist or program can't guarantee that your teenager will turn around and stop rebelling.

If and when intervention is needed, don't let guilt keep you from taking action. Placing a teenager out of the home, for example, doesn't mean you're giving up on her or on your parenting responsibilities. Decisions like these come with prayer and wise counsel from people you trust. It's an emotional time, but the decision needs to be a logical one. And yes, that's easier said than done.

Get support for yourself. Join a sympathetic, small group of parents and bring your pains. Talk with your pastor or mentor. Journal. Do whatever's healthy that will help you through this hard time. That's not being selfish; it's being responsible. Other children, your spouse, or your employer—if you have them—need you to be as sane and healthy as you can be.

Seek professional therapy if needed. If your teenager is in a program where family therapy is recommended or required, participate as fully as you can.

Sometimes all you can do is limit your losses or do damage control, minimizing the effect of your teen's behavior on the rest of the family until he turns 18 and you can escort him out of your house. This may sound harsh, but I don't mean it that way. Sometimes it's just reality.

Do what you can—not what you can't.

As cold as this may sound, weigh the financial cost, too. Even the best program can't guarantee a positive outcome. Don't sink the entire family financially to "save" one family member.

I know that sounds tough. But I've known parents who mortgaged their house to send their teenager to a quality program, strapping the family so much that younger siblings couldn't participate in sports or musical activities because the money wasn't there. In the end, paying for the program created more problems for the entire family than it attempted to solve. It's hard for a parent to think straight when his or her own flesh and blood is involved; that's why godly counsel is so important and necessary.

This leads us to what may be the hardest question of all. Parents often ask, "Will my son (or daughter) ever turn around? What are the chances?"

When I hear this, I know it's not an intellectual "Give me the numbers" question. It's a heartfelt "Give me hope" plea.

The answer I always give is, "I don't know."

But I follow it with what I *do* know:

- It's not your fault.
- Your teen has made his or her own choices, for reasons known or unknown.
- All the work, time, and intervention you've put into this teenager of yours increases the odds that he or she finally will come around.

God is bigger than these problems. That may sound like a cliché, but there's no time for clichés when your teenager is heading down a path of self-destruction. I really mean that God is bigger. Yes, He will allow your teenager to choose stupid. Yet He is interested in the life and salvation of your son or daughter. He sees and knows. And He's bigger than all the stupid choices, dangerous behaviors, and pain.

I have personally witnessed the "coming around" of many teenagers. Some sooner, some later. Many do come back. They really do.

I know it's hard to be the parent of a prodigal, standing at the end of the fence, waiting, waiting, waiting. That's why, in addition to intervening as needed, getting support for yourself is so important.

ELEVEN

"But I'm 18!"

On that magical—or fateful—day your teenager turns 18, the world shudders. In a sense, you officially "lose control." But you don't necessarily like it.

In one moment, much of your world changes. And much of your world stays the same.

No wonder this can be an awkward time for teen and parent. It doesn't have to be, but often it is. Why? How can we make the transition less bumpy?

What Stays the Same

You may expect everything to change when your son or daughter reaches 18, but several key components of life remain the same.

Your primary job as a mom or dad—nurturing or validating—is the same. How you do that job has changed as your child has grown, and it will change again. But the job doesn't.

It's still not your task to make sure your son or daughter turns out "right." His or her new role as an adult doesn't alter what's *not* your job.

The principles of control versus influence don't change:

- What's yours is the same.
- What belongs to your teenager is the same.
- What you can control is the same.
- What you can't control is the same.

The Three Rules of Life remain. Your adult son or daughter will still live or die by individual choices, still has the right to choose smart or stupid, and still faces consequences (the "ouch" part of life) that follow choosing stupid.

You may not be the giver of the "ouch" anymore, but you're still in a position to see your teen hurt by his or her foolishness—and it still grieves you.

The definition and purpose of rules remain the same. The actual rules may change, as we'll see later in this chapter, but the reason for them is the same: "To keep safety in and chaos out."

It's still your house; it's still your rules. If the names on the mortgage, the car loan, and the bank account are the same, it's still your money. It's still your say-so.

All these things remain the same. That may provide a little familiar territory on which to stand while you handle the things that have changed. Solid ground always helps you keep your balance.

Things That Change

Some major things *do* change the moment your teenager moves from being a minor to being a legal adult. The rest of this chapter is about these changes and ways to make the transition a bit easier—or at least a bit less confusing—for you.

While your primary job as a parent stays the same, your *role* changes. You move from guiding to advising or mentoring. Your assignment for the past 18 years—"raising" that son or daughter—has been completed.

Sometimes this transition is easy, sometimes not. An easier transition depends on recognizing that it's coming and cooperating with it—instead of letting it surprise you, seemingly without warning. It may be more complicated if the 18-year-old is the baby of the family, because that means your mothering or fathering days have come to an end. This "unemployment" can be especially difficult if you've been a stay-at-home mom all this time. It can initiate an identity crisis—with questions like, "What do I do now?"

The words you use to refer to your son or daughter may need to change. I often hear parents call an adult son or daughter a "child," but he or she is an adult. Try using "young adult"—or a first name, as you do with other grown-ups in your social circle. Certain family nicknames may still be appropriate, but let your young adult decide. Ask him or her what's acceptable.

Liability has changed. You're no longer officially liable for what your 18-year-old does. Nor are you legally obligated to feed, clothe, house, or finance him or her. The law finally recognizes that you can't control (or be genuinely responsible for) your teen's actions.

Your relationship with your 18-year-old has changed. What was once vertical, parent-to-child, is now horizontal, peer-to-peer, adult-to-adult, equal-to-equal. In many states you may have no legal authority over your son or daughter. This change often frightens parents most; they don't have control, or the perception of control, anymore.

Of course there are some things parents *wish* would change. They find themselves saying, "I wish he would start acting like a responsible adult now," or "I wish she would grow up and take her job and studies seriously instead of still acting like a teeny-bopper."

In time . . . in time.

So what's a parent to do? Let's look at several common situations parents have brought to me regarding their adult sons and daughters. You'll see that a key to success is clearly identifying what's yours and what isn't.

How the Rules Change

To review: Rules aren't for changing behavior or attitudes. They're to keep safety in and chaos out. Regulations dealing with your belongings (house, car, computer, etc.) may remain intact. Those that apply directly to your teenager may need to change.

I once talked with Giselle, mother of Trisha, a 19-year-old college student. Trisha was home for the summer after her first year away. Working a full-time job, she was acting very independently of the rest of the family.

Giselle and her husband, Joe, tried to enforce several rules on Trisha. They included a curfew and going to church with the family. Giselle said the point was to make Trisha "engage with the family . . . like it used to be."

Trisha wasn't cooperating. Giselle called me in a panic: "What do we do?"

After we discussed the lists of things that stay the same and the things that change, Giselle felt better. But she couldn't quite see how to put the concepts into practice.

So I tried a little role-playing. I asked Giselle to pretend I was a single college student renting a room in her home. Would she have any rules for me? If so, what would they be?

She came up with the following:

- When you enter the house at night (with no set time limit), do so quietly and without disrupting others in the house who are sleeping (a chaos issue).
- Keep your personal belongings picked up in the family areas— living room, kitchen, bathroom, and recreation room (another chaos issue).
- No alcohol or illegal drugs may be used or brought into the house or onto the property (a safety issue).

• No pets. (They had more than enough pets, so this was indeed a chaos issue.)

Did Giselle see the need to make *me* attend church every Sunday with her family? Did she require that I observe a curfew? No, because I was not her "child." I encouraged her to look at Trisha in a similar light—a college-age adult boarding for the summer.

As we talked, Giselle realized she was still trying to "mother" Trisha, partly out of worry but mostly out of habit. Giselle had been mothering Trisha for 18 years, a deeply ingrained pattern that was hard to break.

The Boundary Business

Imagine I was renting a room from you, and that you'd given me the same four rules as Giselle's. Yesterday you found six hamsters I'm keeping in my room as pets. What will you now do as my "landlord"?

You'd probably restate the "no pets" rule clearly. You'd tell me I'm in violation of this rule that I agreed to. You'd give me one, two, or seven days to come into "compliance" with the rule.

Or else . . . or else what?

Say it.

I'd have to *leave*.

It wouldn't be your job to find homes for my hamsters. It wouldn't be your job to parent me, though you might use the situation as a mentoring opportunity if our relationship allowed it. It wouldn't be your job to change me or to change your rules to accommodate my whims.

It would have nothing to do with whether you like me, or whether you like hamsters. It's business. It's an adult-to-adult way of handling the issue. I have to comply with your rules or look for a place that *will* accept pets. It's that simple, and it's not personal.

You can't make me comply with the rules. But it's not your job to make me comply; that would be trying to control something that's not yours to control and would border on manipulation. If the rule is a sound one, set in place to keep safety in and chaos out, and I break it—you confront me. If I comply, I can stay if you choose to allow me to stay. It's your house, after all. If I don't comply, you ask me to leave.

And if I refuse to leave willingly, what will you do? Call the police and have me evicted.

That's the way it needs to be with your adult son or daughter, too. That's enforcing healthy boundaries. It's taking control over what's yours without trying to control what's mine.

I realize that when you're dealing with your own flesh and blood, emotions get involved quickly. Take the time to sort out your feelings and deal with the situation in the wisest, most logical manner possible. Pick your dance carefully—and be sure to pick a healthy one.

What About the Car?

Many parents add their teenagers to an existing auto insurance policy as second or third drivers. Even a teenager's "own" car might be titled in a parent's name for insurance reasons. We did that twice. During one period of my life I was the proud owner of four vehicles—and a two-car garage!

An arrangement like this might work until your young adult turns 21—provided he or she is responsible, trustworthy, and cooperative in sharing a "family" vehicle. And it makes having a car more affordable for your son or daughter.

But as a mom I'll call Bonnie asked me, "What do I do when Rianna, my 19-year-old daughter, *demands* the use of my car? She throws a total fit if I don't let her have it. One time she even took the car after I told her no because I had to drive her younger brother to soccer practice. She left me stranded without a car."

I asked this mom, "What would you do if *I* 'borrowed' your car without asking?"

I then got the rest of the story. Rianna had a history of self-mutilating behavior and running away when she didn't get her way. Bonnie was scared that Rianna would do something drastic to hurt herself again, and therefore she wouldn't set any limits or boundaries with her daughter.

You see where this is going, don't you?

Who's in control of Mom's house and vehicle?

Rianna is.

But whose name is on the mortgage and title?

Mom's (and her husband's).

Whose car is it?

Mom's.

So who's the rule-setter supposed to be?

Mom.

I presented Bonnie with two options:

1. She could continue doing the "TOSS and GRAB" dance (see Chapter 5) and let her anxiety determine her interactions with Rianna. She could keep trying to control Rianna's cutting and running away by giving Rianna whatever she wanted.

2. She could set *and enforce* a limit. "It's my car, and you will ask before you take it—or else you will have to find another place to live." She would have to realize that Rianna might choose to do something stupid (Rule Two in action), like actually leaving home.

The choices are clear, but not always easy to act on. In this case, Bonnie was so invested in being the codependent, the GRABer, the "I'll handle it" person, that she did the same thing over and over, somehow hoping for a different outcome.

This mom was afraid, trying to control what was not hers to control, and make her daughter "behave." It didn't work.

It's your car; it's your rules.

"Oh, but A.J.'s car *is* his car," a dad told me. "He bought it with his own money—even though it's in my name for insurance purposes—and he drives it around with expired plates."

I explained to this dad that since it was A.J.'s car, it was A.J.'s responsibility. I also explained that if the dad was liable because his name was on the title, he had the following options:

1. Let A.J. eventually get ticketed for the expired plates and let him pick up the cost of getting them current. If A.J. complies and covers the cost of any penalties, all is well. Rule Three has left a positive impact, at least on his wallet.

2. If A.J. won't cooperate and get the plates current, and you're at risk of liability, transfer the title to A.J.'s name so you have no liability. He would have to get his own insurance coverage as well. But that's his problem, not yours.

3. If A.J. won't pay for current plates, you can sell his car that's in your name and give him the cash from the sale. It would be up to him to get another vehicle, this time in his own name and with his own insurance.

I reminded this dad that these solutions weren't meant to manipulate A.J. into behaving or punish him for misbehaving. This is just life—Rule Three in action. It's the "ouch" of foolish choices. It's also protecting yourself and your own assets.

This dad replied, "There's no way he can afford a car payment, much less insurance for a car in his own name."

"And your point is?" I asked. "Whose problem is that?"

There was no option that guaranteed, "Do this and all will turn out the way you want." But the guy with the gold does make the rules. Again, that's life. Fight reality and you'll lose.

A.J. was between a rock and a hard place. He could follow his dad's rules, get the car registered and up-to-date, and continue to follow his dad's directives about keeping the vehicle legal—thereby keeping the car and the insurance coverage (smart choice). Or he could defy the rules and lose the privilege of "owning" a car that was under Dad's umbrella of insurance coverage (stupid choice).

Either way, it was A.J.'s choice.

It had nothing to do with how much Dad cared for A.J. It wasn't about love. It was about what a parent is to do and not do. And it was okay.

When issues like this arise, examine your motives. Are you . . .

- trying to secretly—or not so secretly—manipulate or force your young adult to behave the way you want him or her to?
- attempting to control things that aren't yours to control?
- trying to "prove" that you really do love your son or daughter?
- trying to change your young adult?
- living "one generation back," perhaps attempting to right a wrong from your own childhood?

Or do your actions reflect a healthy influencing attempt? Are you allowing the "ouch" consequence of a stupid choice to affect him or her?

Check yourself. Review applicable chapters of this book in order to keep the principles fresh—and your mind sane.

Job, School, or Being a "Bum"

Vanessa was totally frustrated. "Michael won't help me at all with any of the chores around the house. He won't go out and get a job. He won't go to school. He just lies around my house, eats all my food, makes a huge mess, watches TV, and expects me to clean up after him. What do I do with this child?"

"How old is Michael?" I asked.

"Oh, he's 42 years old, and he won't—"

Stop! What's wrong with this picture?

Vanessa's situation is a composite of *many* actual stories I've heard in my years of doing therapy. It's more common than you think. Honest.

What's the dance here?

Vanessa gripes to, works for, lectures, pleads with, begs, rages at—and feels needed by—her "child" day after week after year.

Michael puts up with his mother's badgering, is irresponsible, eats Mom out of house and home, and gets free room and board.

Can you see the dance? Michael TOSSes and Vanessa GRABs.

Okay, you're the therapist now. What would you recommend to Vanessa? That she kick Michael out? Imagine how hard it would be for a parent to put his or her "child" onto the street "with no place to go."

We'll get back to this kind of situation later in this chapter.

In the meantime, consider Alex. He was 23, a recent college graduate who'd returned to live with his parents until he got "established." But Alex couldn't seem to find a suitable position in his field. He seemed depressed much of the time, lacking motivation for job hunting. He'd sleep until 11:30 A.M., do some online searching for employment, and call it quits for the day after submitting one or two resumés or applications.

Alex's parents contacted me after dealing with this for eight months.

"What do we do?" they asked. Neither parent felt it was wise to kick Alex out on the street, but they didn't want to encourage his behavior, either.

"He's a great kid," Mom told me as Dad nodded in agreement.

After I collected the pertinent history and met with Alex, it became clear that he—like many firstborns—was very perfectionistic and anxiety-prone. The world of "after college"—the real world—was so overwhelming and scary to him that he shut down. Or froze up.

Kicking Alex out in the name of tough love wouldn't have been the best way to address the situation. Instead, I helped set him up with a job-search coordinator and a career counselor.

I also gave him homework assignments like creating a budget and role-playing job interviews. We worked on his perfectionistic patterns, and used thought-stopping techniques to slow his anxious thinking.

Alex's problem wasn't rebelliousness or irresponsibility—as it was in Michael's case. Alex's unhealthy "brain freeze," a result of feeling overwhelmed and anxious about big-world decisions, was paralyzing him.

Slowly, with assistance, Alex landed a good job and was able to move into his own place.

(Whew!)

As I think about these cases, I remember the wear and tear the parents suffered. Let me encourage you—again—to rally support around yourself during times like these. Reach out to trusted family members or friends; contact your pastor, youth pastor, or on-staff counselor. Talk with the counselor at your teenager's school, if that applies. If need be, pay a professional counselor for advice and suggestions.

It's your parental heart that's heavy; take care of it. It's your parental brain that's feeling fuzzy and on the verge of going crazy; take care of it.

Keep caring about your son or daughter, and about yourself, too. It's not wrong or selfish. It's smart.

College Money

I know this makes me sound old, but back in *my* day most college-bound students seemed willing to do whatever it took to get their degrees. It didn't matter whether they had to go part-time or full-time, win scholarships or take out loans, or work their way through. If Mom and Dad could help out, great.

Now there seems to be a different attitude. There's "no way" to get to college unless Mom and Dad foot the bill. The prevailing wish also seems to be, "I want to go *away* to college." This usually means higher costs, thanks to out-of-state tuition or private college fees.

If Mom and Dad don't—or can't—fund the college "experience" (when did a college education become an "experience," anyway?), there's no other option. Somehow we parents have become *obligated* to pay.

Don't fall for this thinking or pressure. If your son or daughter is headed for college, you're *not* obligated to pay for it. You may *choose* to pay, or to help pay. That would be fine. But it's your money; it's your say-so.

Besides, there are ways to get a college education without any assistance from parents. It may not be the "experience" your teenager was hoping for, and it may take longer, but it's still possible.

If you do want to help your collegian with educational expenses, consider these ideas that have helped other parents:

1. Make sure this is in your son's or daughter's best interest, not yours. Be careful not to live one generation back—trying to make up for the education you didn't get, or to turn your teen into a family trophy.

2. Realize the academic arena is not suited for everyone. Pursue what will best fit your young adult in the long run.

3. Don't use your money to attempt to control or manipulate your collegian's life and behaviors. I hear this one over and over from students and parents alike.

I was presenting a lecture about parenting teenagers to 88 students, mostly college juniors and seniors. When we got to the part about school and money, the class lit up. Many students said they felt pushed, forced, manipulated, and "guilted" by their parents' checkbooks. Here are just a few of their stories:

- "Dad makes me feel guilty if I don't call Mom every week. After all, he says, they are paying out so much money for my education; at least I could call her."

- "My parents refused to help pay for any of my education unless I went to the specific university they chose for me—their alma mater. It was a 'family pride' thing for them to have at least one of their children graduate from there and keep the family heritage going."

- "I wanted to take last summer and travel through Europe with some friends, but Dad said he wouldn't pay for my senior year if I didn't come home and work at his business over the summer."

From the parents' side, I've heard of similar actions that seem like efforts to control their collegians' choices:

- "If Susan won't go to a Christian college, then I'm not paying a penny for her education. The only good education is a Christian education."

- "I told Mitch that we weren't going to pay another semester of his college until he broke up with his non-Christian girlfriend."

These stories are true.

Yes, it's your money and your say-so. But what's your motive? Are you trying to buy your son's or daughter's behavior? Are you trying to make his life turn out the way you want? Are you trying to play the role of God? These are important questions to ask yourself.

I've gone through this twice myself. Here are some suggestions based on my experience and that of many other parents.

First, determine ahead of time—preferably before your son's or daughter's senior year of high school—how much money, if any, you can afford to put toward a college education. Set a specific dollar amount for each year.

"We'll pay for college" is too vague. What if your student wants to go to England and attend Oxford University? The more specific you are, the better everyone will understand the plan.

Next, create a "Mom and Pop Scholarship Fund" that will pay that set amount per semester for a certain number of semesters. This doesn't have to be a contract; just make sure it's well understood by all parties. If your teenager chooses a college that costs *less* per semester than the fund provides, you can decide whether to allow the balance of the money to go toward a laptop, grad school, an overseas educational opportunity, a summer mission trip, or something else.

If the chosen college costs *more* than the scholarship amount, it's up to your son or daughter to come up with the difference—through other scholarships, loans, or employment. It's not your job to "fix" the deficit. If your student doesn't come up with the difference—well, I guess he'll have to reconsider his school choice, won't he?

That's life. That's the way it is. This approach teaches your collegian the ways of the adult world—a lesson as important as any in physics or engineering.

Finally, operate your "Mom and Pop Scholarship Fund" like a real one. While such funds might not have "strings" attached, they often require that students meet certain standards to take possession of the money—such as maintaining a sufficient grade point average and to work toward a degree. In the same way, make sure your requirements are attached to measurable educational performance—not your teenager's personal behavior.

Mitch's dad told me he wouldn't keep paying his son's tuition unless the young man broke up with his girlfriend. He was trying to buy his son's behavior, not purchase a good education. Mitch was averaging a 4.0 GPA—in electrical engineering, no less.

I challenged that dad by asking, "What are you buying with your money? Are you buying an education for your son so he can get a good start in life? Or are you buying—or attempting to buy—your future daughter-in-law?"

Be careful to understand the motives behind your use of money. Make the "Mom and Pop Scholarship Fund" contingent on things like these:

- a 3.0 cumulative GPA (or whatever you deem appropriate)
- courses that move toward a degree
- enrollment for eight (or whatever number) semesters

These requirements are tied to purchasing a good education for your student—nothing more.

The rest is now up to your son or daughter. If he or she meets the requirements, the money is available. If not, he or she goes on "academic probation" with one semester to raise the GPA to the required level. If that doesn't happen, he or she loses the scholarship and will have to come up with other money until getting back into compliance.

It's up to your student to fix this problem, not you. It's a way for your son or daughter to experience the grown-up world—though that could mean a baptism by fire. It's also a good reminder that the money is not endless or to be used to take a collection of "fun" classes only. It's for an education that can be used to get a job and pay one's own way.

At the end of the predetermined semesters, your "Mom and Pop Scholarship Fund" expires. If you choose to offer additional assistance in the form of a "Mom and Pop Scholarship Fund, Part II," that's up to you. It's your money; it's yours to offer (or not).

That's how most scholarships operate. It's not personal. It's the Three Rules of Life.

This approach lessens the stress for you *and* your teen. It makes life a little easier when you know what's yours to control and what isn't.

As a matter of fact, you might even consider this approach even if you *do* have all the funds for your teen's higher education. As the old saying goes, "Nobody ever flunked a course he paid for out of his own pocket." Requiring your son or daughter to pay a portion may provide an even better educational experience than getting a full ride.

"But our kid doesn't want to work even though he has lots of free time," some parents might say. "He still expects us to pay all his college and living expenses. Do we pay for everything since he's not working, or what?"

It's your money; it's your choice. You're not *obligated* to pay for college *or* living expenses. You may choose to, but it's not a requirement for the "good parent" club. If your student can work—even though he'd rather not—why not pay for his tuition and let him pay for books and living expenses? If he can work, have him work.

You have to work and pay your way. So do I. Your student can do the same. After all, working is an education, too.

When It's Time to Leave

Sometimes tensions rise beyond a bearable level, even if you've done all the right things as the parent of a young adult.

You don't agree with her foolish choices and irresponsible behavior. You don't condone his attitudes and actions. You don't try to control her or "fix" her problems for her.

But what *do* you do?

If possible, you live with the tension and the differences. But sometimes you can't—or it wouldn't be healthy to do so. What then?

As mean as it may sound—and I don't intend it that way—you can't let one member of the family sink the entire household. There may come a time when the tension is causing damage. It's not safe physically, emotionally, mentally, or spiritually for others in the household. There may come a point where having the young adult in the house brings chaos.

When your teenager is a minor and there are safety or chaos issues, it's necessary to do "damage control." Once he or she is officially an adult, though, there's usually no reason to keep the damage-causer under your roof.

How do you decide whether this point has been reached?

Good—and hard—question.

If you face this dilemma, check your motives first. Why are you ready—or unwilling—to kick your son or daughter out of the house? When in doubt, seek counsel from a pastor or therapist.

Second, as objectively as you can, do a "damage assessment" of the entire family. How is keeping this young adult in your home hurting others? Is the damage serious and permanent? Talk your assessment over with a counselor.

Be sure to account for intangibles as well. These might include the demands on your emotional energy and the focus and time needed to spend on other children—as well as your own sanity. Be practical. You're not superhuman, and neither are others living in your home. Don't expect anyone to endure a relational hurricane just because he or she is "family."

There may come a time when sending the young adult out on his or her own is the better thing to do.

John and Betty were in this very spot. Their daughter, Porscha, was living in total rebellion against legitimate household rules, putting up unacceptable posters and wearing offensive T-shirts, overtly defying her parents. Porscha was the oldest of four, and her behavior had a negative impact on the other children. Betty was short-tempered with all the kids because of her anger toward her eldest; John couldn't give the other children the time and attention they needed, occupied as he was with "putting out fires" Porscha kept igniting.

John and Betty wanted me to "talk some sense into Porscha." After listening to them, I told them it wasn't so much Porscha's "issue" (believe me, she had her share) as it was theirs. They agreed to meet with me themselves.

As I laid out their options—one of which was putting their daughter out of the house—Betty blurted, "Oh, no, we can't do that! She'll go and live with her boyfriend then, and that would be just awful."

Whose job was it to make sure Porscha lived a moral life?

Porscha's.

Who was trying to control the situation to make sure Porscha didn't live an immoral life?

Betty. She was GRABing, and Porscha was happy to TOSS.

See the dance here? Much of the chaos in the household stemmed from Betty's attempt to control something she couldn't—Porscha. The other major ingredient was Betty's anxiety, one of the big stumbling blocks in the parenting process.

Principle: *Don't make decisions based on fear.* Yes, it's okay to feel anxious. Realize it, name it, but don't let it become the deciding factor. If you do, you'll almost always make a poor choice. It will be based not on solving the problem but on avoiding what you're afraid of.

John and Betty's situation is similar to many I've worked with. Often it's the father who's ready to kick the young adult out—because he's fed up and tends to handle things in a more businesslike fashion. Mom is more often the parent worried about the "child's" safety and feelings.

One position isn't right and the other wrong; they can actually create a good balance for each other.

This was the case with another couple I worked with recently. Mario was ready to "call the police" and have them "drag" his son away. He had "absolutely no tolerance" for anybody who wouldn't do exactly what he ordered when he ordered it.

Amanda, his wife, was worried for their 22-year-old son—and hurt because she thought Mario's message to their son was that he didn't love him. She also was bitter toward Mario because he worked all the time and left parenting chores and follow-through to her.

Trying to keep emotions under control and foster a wise and cooperative decision, I encouraged Mario and Amanda to follow this three-step process:

1. As individuals, write a personal list of the statements you want to communicate clearly to your son.

2. As a couple, review each other's lists and develop an *agreed upon* list of statements. This is a key point, because if both parents don't agree on this action step, it won't work. Disagreement also will cause even more tension in the marriage than is already being created by the conflict with the young adult. In this case, the final statement was something like, "You have 10 days to pack your stuff up and relocate." Mario wanted to add, "Or I'm calling the police!" I encouraged him not to, because it wasn't necessary. If the son refused to leave, Mario could calmly call the police to have his son escorted off the premises. It wasn't necessary to say so up front.

3. After a joint list is agreed upon, sit down as a couple with the young adult and say or read the statements.

I suggest this process to any couple—or single parent—facing a similar situation. Remember, though, that follow-through is vital. If your son or daughter won't meet the criteria for staying in your home, you'll need to calmly call the police. If you're not willing or able to make that call, don't give him or her the eviction notice.

You don't have to start with the police. If you think your son or daughter may cooperate in the presence of other people from your church, neighborhood, or community, you could have a non-family member there on eviction day. If that doesn't work, you'll need to call the police to have your young adult escorted off the premises.

Making a stand as just described isn't designed to scare the young adult into compliance. That's manipulation, and it won't work in the long run. Sons and daughters get evicted because their behaviors and actions earned it. It's their fault, their problem to fix—not yours.

"But my 18-year-old son is still in high school," Carrie protested as she sat in my office. "There's no way I can kick him out."

Carrie knew David really wanted to graduate with his high school class. She knew if he left home, he'd live with his narcissistic father—who didn't really care about David but would use him to hurt Carrie. She also knew it would be devastating for David to be uprooted from the church youth group; he was even being mentored by the youth pastor and his wife.

But Carrie also knew it wasn't working to have her son under her roof. That didn't change just because her 18-year-old adult son was still in high school.

I asked whether Carrie knew anybody in her church who'd be willing to give David room and board for the eight months until graduation. She went looking and praying. In the end, we relocated David to the home of a church member.

This kind of setup doesn't work very often, but it did in Carrie's case. David stayed involved with the youth group, finished high school, graduated, and became more responsible for himself. He surprised Carrie and me by actually developing a healthy relationship and friendship with his mother.

Still, many of these situations don't turn out "happily ever after." One single mother had to put her 19-year-old son out of her home even though he didn't have a place to go. She rented an inexpensive motel room for four weeks, helped her son pack and move, then left him to be responsible for himself. It cost her some precious money, but she did what she needed to do.

To my knowledge, the relationship never mended. She was a hurting mom, but at least she was free from the guilt and feelings of responsibility for her son's actions.

Love Can Be Tough

There's nothing magical about the number 18. It's simply the age at which, in a number of ways, a change in the balance of power and legal obligation takes place. The transition may go smoothly, or it may not.

When it doesn't, and a tough-love action like kicking your young adult out of the home is the wisest option available, it's hard. But sometimes we parents are called upon to do the hard and wise thing.

At times like this you'll want to seek outside counsel. Talk to your pastor, a mentor couple, your cell group. Ask people you trust to join you in praying for wisdom and strength. Take care of yourself, too.

I hope you never have to use the more difficult advice in this chapter. But if you do, remember:

Do what you can, not what you can't.

And base your decisions on what's right, wise, and healthy—not on what you fear.

TWELVE

Bringing It All Home

It's time for the Losing Control 101 final exam. Let's see whether the principles presented in this book have stuck in your mind. If not, don't worry; you'll find the answers at the end of the test.

1. What's the primary job of a dad in raising teenagers?
>A. Pay for everything.
>B. Go to dance performances and soccer games.
>C. Validate each of your children.
>D. All of the above.

2. What's the primary job of a mom in raising teenagers?
>A. Nurture each of your children.
>B. Drive everyone to dance performances and soccer games.
>C. Keep the house clean and tidy.
>D. All of the above.

3. What's *not* your job as a parent?
>A. Make sure they turn out "right."
>B. Make sure they turn out "right."
>C. Make sure they turn out "right."
>D. All of the above.

4. **Which of the following is *not* one of the Three Rules of Life?**
    A. You live and die by your own choices.
    B. You can choose smart or you can choose stupid.
    C. It's okay as long as you don't get caught.
    D. There's always somebody or something whose job is to make your life miserable when you choose stupid.

5. **Which word means to have direct and complete power over?**
    A. responsible
    B. liable
    C. control
    D. influence

6. **Which word means to be legally bound to make good any loss or damage?**
    A. responsible
    B. liable
    C. control
    D. influence

7. **Which word means to take ownership of, or able to respond to?**
    A. responsible
    B. liable
    C. control
    D. influence

8. **Which word means to affect, impress, bias, sway, or inspire?**
    A. responsible
    B. liable
    C. control
    D. influence

9. **In the following "dances," identify the styles of relating that both parent and teen are using.**

A. TEEN: "Mom, you have to take me to school right now! Let's go!"

PARENT: "Why?"

TEEN: "Because the bus left without me, and you didn't iron anything for me to wear, and your hair dryer doesn't work, and if I'm late one more time to Mr. Anderson's class I'll get suspended!"

PARENT: "Well, you'll have to ride your bike, I guess, because I have to take your brother to his physical therapy appointment in 30 minutes."

TEEN: "Aauugghh! You love him and so hate me! I can't believe this! I hate this life!"

PARENT: "Your bike's in the garage, Honey. Be sure to take a lock with you."

B. PARENT: "Son, you broke your mother's heart. You need to go in there right now and apologize!"

TEEN: "I already talked with Mom and worked it out."

PARENT: "That's not good enough. Until you stop bringing her car back totally out of gas, you're going to have to check her keys in and out through me."

TEEN: "But it's all settled. I even gave her a twenty and washed her car this afternoon."

PARENT: "Until I know you'll never bring her car back low on gas again, you'll report to me. As long as you're in my house, you do what I tell you. Is that clear?"

10. **What's the key word or phrase for perfectionistic thinking?**
    A. "Now that's the right way to do something!"
    B. "If you want something done right, you've got to do it yourself."
    C. "If you aren't going to do your best, then don't do it at all."
    D. "I should . . ." or "You shouldn't . . ."

11. **What's the key phrase for anxious or worried thinking?**
    A. "Eeeeek!"
    B. "I don't know . . ."
    C. "What if . . ."
    D. "The sky is falling, the sky is falling!"

12. **Anger is a mix of _____ and _____.**
    A. hurt and disappointment
    B. bad chips and salsa
    C. hurt and worry
    D. boredom and frustration

13. **Which of the following describe the reasons for rules?**
    A. to keep your blood pressure down
    B. to keep safety in
    C. to keep chaos out
    D. to change your teenager's attitude

14. **Which of the following is *not* a principle to consider when deciding on a consequence for a broken rule?**
    A. Make sure they never do it again.
    B. You need to be able to enforce the consequence.
    C. Consequences need to be clear and limited in length.
    D. Tie an "attitude change" to getting the privilege back.

15. **Which items stay the same when your son or daughter turns 18?**
    A. the Three Rules of Life
    B. your primary job as a parent
    C. the names on the mortgage, the car loan, and your bank account
    D. the things you can and can't control

16. **Which items *change* when your son or daughter turns 18?**
    A. his or her maturity level
    B. your liability for your teenager
    C. your role as a parent
    D. the balance of power between the two of you

ANSWERS

1. C	10. D
2. A	11. C
3. D	12. C
4. C	13. B, C
5. C	14. A, D
6. B	15. A, B, C, D
7. A	16. B, C, D
8. D	

9. A. Teen=TOSSer
    Parent=FOLDer
  B. Parent=GRABer
    Teen=HOLDer

You Can Do It

You can control yourself—what you do, think, and believe, and how you manage your feelings.

You can't control what your teenager does, thinks, or believes, or how he handles his emotions.

It's not your job, either.

You *can* influence, teach, mentor, correct, discipline, and make stupid choices "ouch" for your teenager.

But you can't make her turn out "right."

That's not your job. Nor is it your fault if she chooses poorly.

Losing control—or the illusion of control you never really had—is not easy. We like our illusions, especially when it comes to controlling our children.

In our control-freak society, we come face-to-face with the age-old spiritual struggle of surrender. I don't hear surrender preached about much nowadays, but it's still part of spiritual maturity. If I asked you on Sunday who's in charge of looking out for your teenager—you or God—you'd probably know the "right" answer and say, "God." What you might not say out loud is, "As long as He keeps my son safe the way I want Him to."

Just a few days ago I talked about this with a mom I'll call Sarah. She *wants* to be responsible for the safety of her 16-year-old son, Luke. Why? Because then things will turn out the way she wants them to—or so her illusion goes.

She wants God to be the One who looks out for Luke's best interests—as long as He does it according to her specifications. In Sarah's theology, God is sovereign and that's "okay" with her—almost as if God needs her permission. In everyday life, though, *she* wants that position of sovereign control—at least when it comes to her son.

Sarah called me because her illusion of control had just been shattered. So had her illusion that her prayers could make God do as she wished—namely, keep Luke "safe." She wanted her illusions back. She wanted control over Luke's life. She wanted to take Luke to counseling and get things back the way they "used to be"—back into her nice, tidy, illusion-filled way of seeing the world.

As we talked, I pressed Sarah with questions:

"Who's the one really in charge of Luke—you or God?"

"Is God really sovereign all the time, or only on Sundays?"

"Why did God allow Adam and Eve to eat from the forbidden tree? Why didn't He stop them?"

"If God really is in charge, why are you trying to tell Him how best to handle things with Luke? Isn't that sort of playing God, in effect making God your genie in a bottle and telling Him how to run the world of 'Luke'?"

Sarah wrestled with my questions. But when she replied, it was like this: "Luke is my son, and I don't want him to get hurt. I want to be sure he stays safe [by my criteria]."

Notice the pronouns in Sarah's thinking?

Losing control—even the perception of control—of your teenager and what may befall him or her can be scary. Yet it's also freeing. And it's better for you . . . and for him or her.

Keeping the legitimate control you do have is an empowering thing. That's also good for both of you, even though your teen may beg to differ.

One Last Way to Influence

One trick of the trade I use when working with teenagers (and others) is asking questions. It's an art and a science. It doesn't come naturally with knowing how to talk. Good question-asking takes practice and thought.

Questions almost always go further than answers—making statements—when you're trying to influence. Sometimes you need to make statements and give answers. But when you can, engage your teenager by asking questions.

Don't make it an interrogation: "Where were you on the night of September 23, at 7:23?" Instead, use conversational queries that encourage dialogue. Here's why:

- Questions encourage teenagers to think for themselves. You don't want an automatic "Yes, Sir" response (which most teenagers won't give anyway unless it's dripping with 36 pounds of sarcasm). Questions help them learn to think logically and critically. You want to teach them to fish, not just give them a fish.

- Questions often help keep the conversation going more than statements do. A well-asked question can ease the defensiveness that greets an "answer."

- Questions help you remember that you want to influence, not control. They can remind you of the limits of your power.

- Questions invite conversation without forcing or manipulating your teenager—if they're asked correctly.

- Questions tend to slow down your own thinking and tendencies to prejudge a situation. You can try to collect the necessary data by asking questions.

- Questions tend to linger in the mind of your teenager longer than answers do. An answer sounds like, ". . .the land of the free . . . and the home . . . of the brave." It's the end of the song. A question sounds like, "Happy birthday to you. Happy birthday to—" Your brain doesn't like being left hanging, so it wants to finish the song. That's the way it is with questions; they leave your teenager hanging on to what you just asked, even if he or she shrugs a shoulder and says, "I don't know." The question's still there, hanging, and you've just increased your influencing power tenfold.

You can even ask a question when you want to give advice. Make an observation and end it with a question. Here's what I mean:

- "Whenever you're hanging with Jimmy, you seem to be uptight, stressed, and sad a whole lot more. Do you notice that?"
- "When you sign up for those exotic summer trips to Europe, the deposit is usually nonrefundable. Have you asked whether it's refundable or not and when the deadline is to get your money back if necessary?"
- "You look like you're not getting enough sleep during the week, Honey. Do you feel that tired? Do you think you're getting enough rest?"

No, it's not "reverse psychology" or manipulation or mental gymnastics. It's just asking good questions while introducing an observation. Practice this, and it can take you a long way toward increasing your influence with your teenager.

It also helps to put facts into forms that encourage your teen to consider them—not just swallow them. When I offer an observation, I often start like this:

- "I wonder if . . ."
- "Do you think maybe . . ."
- "Could it be that . . ."
- "Just an idea—what do you think of . . ."

Facts are facts. But teenagers can choose to buy into them (smart choice) or not (stupid choice). You want to influence them to consider the facts and choose smart. That's part of what you *can* do—unashamedly, I might add.

This approach keeps the control in their hands. It also makes your job as a parent easier—because it's not up to you to make them "get it."

Let Them Go and They'll Probably Be Back

One of the parents I work with told me about a bumper sticker that read,

> I'VE CHILD-PROOFED MY HOUSE,
> BUT THEY KEEP FINDING THEIR WAY BACK IN!

Losing control of your son or daughter can be a very healthy and fun time. You can start relating as adult to adult, peer to peer, friend to friend, shoe collector to shoe collector, football fan to football fan.

It can be heartwarming to get a cell phone call on your way home from work asking, "What are you having for dinner tonight? Willy and I don't have anything in the apartment to eat."

It can be encouraging beyond words when one of the women in your "girls' night out" group is your daughter. Or, in my case, when two of your mountain-bike-riding buddies are your sons-in-law.

I can't guarantee a happy ending. But I do know that as we let go of our teenagers—let them grow up, let them take the control that really is theirs, and let them live by the truth—usually they come back around and want a healthy friendship with us. Not as your "child," but as individuals.

It may seem hard to believe that your teenager would ever want to spend time with you, but research backs that up. A 2007 poll asked 1,280 young people (ages 13 to 24) about happiness.[1] The number one answer to the question, "What makes you happy?" was "Spending time with family." It wasn't drugs, money, cars, cell phones, or sex. It was being with you.

In the same poll, nearly 75 percent of respondents said their relationship with their parents made them happy. That's good news! Your teenager may never tell you that, but the survey did.

Even with the obstacles, parenting is a doable job. Hang in there. Do what you can, not what you can't.

And when losing control of your teen seems anything but likable, think of Jennifer's story.

I met Jennifer while working at an adolescent treatment center in Colorado some years ago. Behavioral issues had brought her there; she had a rebellious attitude toward her father, a career military officer.

As her father often noted, Jennifer was not a "bad kid." In fact, he said, "She's a great girl. I just don't know why she's doing what she's doing." She was making lots of stupid choices, over and over again.

After working with Jennifer at the center, I was her therapist when she was discharged. Eventually things seemed to be on a healthy track, and we ended therapy.

About a year later, though, I got a call from her father. Jennifer, now 20, was back to making stupid choices—which included breaking the law. Her brokenhearted dad didn't even know where she was. When we ended the conversation, I told him I really believed Jennifer would "come around." I just couldn't say when.

Another year passed. I got another call from Jennifer's father. This time he said Jennifer indeed had come around, cleaning up her legal messes by taking ownership and paying for what she'd done. She'd recently joined the army, wanting some structure in her life and to learn how to accept authority figures.

Jennifer was genuinely sorry for all the grief she'd caused her dad. She told him, "I love you . . . and thank you for not giving up on me when I was such a pain."

The prodigal daughter had returned. The "good kid" was becoming a mature adult. And a dad's broken heart was mending.

That's why I work week in and week out with teenagers and their parents. A whole lot of messed-up teens do come around. And a whole lot of aching parents finally breathe a sigh of relief.

Losing control in a healthy way is worth every minute.

Or to put it another way, in the words of a T-shirt I saw in a quaint little shop on Cape Cod, Massachusetts,

> GRANDCHILDREN: THE REWARD YOU GET
> FOR NOT STRANGLING YOUR TEENAGER.

Amen!

NOTES

Chapter 1

1. The author of this expanded version of the "Serenity Prayer" is unknown; the original, shorter version is generally attributed to Reinhold Niebuhr, who apparently wrote it as early as 1934. Found at http://en.wikipedia.org/wiki/Serenity_Prayer, March 15, 2008.

Chapter 3

1. Grossman, Lev, "They Just Won't Grow Up," *Time*, January 24, 2005, pp. 42-53.
2. Ibid.
3. Ibid.

Chapter 12

1. "Youths' Stuff of Happiness May Surprise Parents," Associated Press, found at http://www.msnbc.msn.com/id/20322621/, August 20, 2007.

FOCUS ON THE FAMILY®

Welcome to the Family

Whether you purchased this book, borrowed it, or received it as a gift, we're glad you're reading it. It's just one of the many helpful, encouraging, and biblically based resources produced by Focus on the Family® for people in all stages of life.

Focus began in 1977 with the vision of one man, Dr. James Dobson, a licensed psychologist and author of numerous best-selling books on marriage, parenting, and family. Alarmed by the societal, political, and economic pressures that were threatening the existence of the American family, Dr. Dobson founded Focus on the Family with one employee and a once-a-week radio broadcast aired on 36 stations.

Now an international organization reaching millions of people daily, Focus on the Family is dedicated to preserving values and strengthening and encouraging families through the life-changing message of Jesus Christ.

Focus on the Family
MAGAZINES

These faith-building, character-developing publications address the interests, issues, concerns, and challenges faced by every member of your family from preschool through the senior years.

FOCUS ON THE FAMILY CITIZEN®
U.S. news issues

FOCUS ON THE FAMILY CLUBHOUSE JR.™
Ages 4 to 8

FOCUS ON THE FAMILY CLUBHOUSE®
Ages 8 to 12

For More
INFORMATION

ONLINE:
Log on to
FocusOnTheFamily.com
In Canada, log on to
FocusOnTheFamily.ca

PHONE:
Call toll-free:
800-A-FAMILY
(232-6459)
In Canada, call toll-free: 800-661-9800

BREAKAWAY®
Teen guys

BRIO®
Teen girls
12 to 15

BRIO & BEYOND®
Teen girls 16 to 19

PLUGGED IN®
Reviews movies, music, TV

Rev. 6/08

More Great Resources
from Focus on the Family®

Sticking with Your Teen
By Joe White and Lissa Halls Johnson
Is your teen resentful? Rebellious? It's time to be relentless! When it comes to mending your relationship, it's never too late to start—and it's always too soon to quit. Find out how to get closer, beginning today—and why there's more hope for your tomorrows than you may have dreamed.

The DNA of Parent-Teen Relationships
By Gary Smalley and Greg Smalley, Psy.D.
You *can* have a great relationship with your teenager, and *The DNA of Parent-Teen Relationships* reveals how! Written by best-selling author Gary Smalley and his son Greg, it focuses on *the* key element that will make any relationship great, and will show you how to forge a strong and lasting bond with your young adult.

Closer
By Susie Shellenberger
Take one part talking, two parts listening, sprinkle liberally with Scripture and fun activities and what do you have? Susie Shellenberger's book *Closer*, written especially for mothers and teen daughters to experience together.